Table of content

1. Introduction
2. Why does the RFP Process need a Major Upgrade?
   2.1   The History
   2.2   A Closer Look at the Evidence
   2.3   The RfP 3.0 „Request for Partici-pation" - A major Upgrade, but NO silver Bullet!
3. Values & Principles of Lean-Agile Procure-ment
   3.1   DAYS instead of MONTHS
   3.2   NEEDS instead of WANTS
   3.3   ADAPTIVE instead of FIXED
   3.4   PARTNERSHIP instead of RELA-TIONSHIP
   3.5   FUN instead of PAIN
4. The Lean Procurement Canvas
   4.1   Where to start & what do all the sections mean?
   4.2   Is one Page really enough for e.g. a $ 1 bn Sourcing Case?

4.3 The Canvas a Risk Mitigation Framework

4.4 Common Pitfalls

4.5 Application Areas for the Canvas

5. Lean-Agile Procurement - A Framework or a new Mindset?

    5.1 Procurement is the Investor for the Organization!

    5.2 Scaling LAP for small & huge Business Cases

    5.3 A Deeper Dive into the LAP Patterns („Steps")

        5.3.1 Initialization

        5.3.2 Preparation

        5.3.3 Execution / Big Room Workshop - How to co-create an Agile Contract in less than 1-2 days with multiple parties?

        5.3.4 Peer-feedback/-decision

6. Case Studies

    6.1 Sourcing of a Group ERP in 2 Days - New World Record!

6.2 How Agile is changing an Industry & Lives!

6.3 Awarded success Story with the Dunedin City Council

6.4 How the Hospital in Stockholm was newly built on Time, on Budget & has also saved Värmland County Council €300 Mio

6.5 FLASH - Learnings from a $1.5 BN Challenged-based Procurement in the US Government

6.6 How Swiss Federal Railways reduced Complexity in Critical Procurement Projects

6.7 General Observations, Recommendations & Opportunities for Government Procurement

6.8 From Fairytales to Agile: How to Source $1 BN new Trains Investment by Applying LAP Full stack

7. Challenges & Solutions applying Lean-Agile Procurement

8. Implement LAP yourself

8.1 Become a Certified LAP Practitioner

8.2   Agile Coaching and/or a Pilot Project

8.3   Starting small - Apply a pattern

9.   Current & Future Trends

9.1   Scaling LAP for small & huge Business Cases

9.2   Agile Partner Management

9.3   Agile Contracts / Agreements

9.4   The future of Procurement: From Function to Capability

9.5   Beyond Supply Chain - Adaptive Partner Ecosystem

Foreword

„An innovative approach to sourcing can bring positive results and if you don't try new approaches then you will never know what might be achieved. Lean Agile Procurement can deliver real value, bring novel solutions, often with a far more collaborative approach, in certain situations. If you already have well developed procurement practices, are faced with a complex sourcing challenge for services, with few suppliers and you are looking for new ways to unlock value then Lean Agile Procurement is an approach you should consider. It will take far less time than traditional sourcing practices and is a great technique for involving both internal stakeholders and suppliers in identifying not just the optimum solution but how to get it implemented.

Three major criticisms of Procurement teams that I hear far too often are ‚They are too slow', ‚They have a controlling not a collaborative mindset' and ‚They don't truly access the innovative solutions which the supply base can offer'. Well, Lean Agile Procurement addresses miro all three of these and in especially in

those categories which most need this approach such as complex services and innovation. In my opinion there is another benefit too. Procurement professionals who experience Lean Agile Procurement will learn new techniques and capabilities which they can then apply to other categories. If you don't try you will never learn."
— **Malcolm Harrison** - former CPO InBev, CPO Nestle, CEO Chartered Institute of Procurement & Supply.

"Thank you Mirko, for this book and the change you're leading. Traditional procurement (sourcing) activity, in my experience, can take too long, is overly restrictive and concentrates overly upon complicated and costly processes that minimise rather than understand and manage risk. The agile concepts Mirko describes, and is extending across the globe, counter this with accelerated, innovative ideas that I have seen deliver improved outcomes for clients (buyers) successful and unsuccessful suppliers.

There is no panacea to great government procurement, but embracing the opportunity and experimenting with the ideas and frameworks Mirko describes is a necessity for the modern procurement professional.
— **Laurence Pidcock** General Manager New Zealand Government Procurement

„Adaptability is a critical competence for survival in today's volatile and unpredictable markets. Given their historical focus on control and compliance, it is also a characteristic that most procurement teams lack.

That is why adopting Lean-Agile Procurement is such an essential step. We do not have time for incremental change. So my recommendation is to read, to learn - and most important, to implement!"

– **Tim Cummins** President World Commerce & Contracting

"Lean at its roots in the "Toyota Production System" is about reducing and eliminating non-value-added activity, typically called waste of the Japanese term muda. The latter is better defined as something senseless or meaningless, also uselessness or futility. Clumsiness and a lack of professionalism leads to unnecessary costs. Everyone has to try to eliminate unnecessary effort or spending.

Agile is a philosophy (a theory or attitude that acts as a guiding principle for behavior) that was encapsulated in the "Agile Manifesto 2001" but has since been coopted by every marketeer and peddler of frameworks and methodologies.

Agility is an emergent property of the way we do work and the way we behave. It enables faster decision making and a bias towards action. It stops debate and focuses on doing.

Too many people are concatenating and conflating Lean-Agile as a terminology for anything they want to sell in the same way the Lean and Six Sigma movement concatenated terminology to create the perception of the new methodology, when the two are very different approaches, one being behavioral and the other statistical.

The challenge here for Mirko was to avoid this trend and to create an original approach in his work to solving procurement headaches that beset all corporate bodies that do business with third parties; so, all of them. I think he has achieved something special that will be of huge value to those that digest and understand the work he has presented. He has created something that focuses on communication and collaboration in a high trust environment. This approach results in both the elimination of non-value-added work as well as creating the conditions for rapid decision making and action. He may just have used Lean and Agile together correctly!

A very worthwhile read and one any leader would benefit from, especially those in procurement, vendor management, finance, and accounting.

—**Nigel Thurlow** CEO – The Flow Consortium, co-creator of The Flow System and creator of Scrum The Toyota Way.

"Why agile procurement is key to Procurement's future - Procurement & Supply Asia / Pacific (PASA) has been committed to the idea of lean agile procurement (LAP), through Mirko and his colleagues of the LAP Alliance particularly, since the first LAP workshop held in Australia back in 2018.

The reason is simple - we believe it is part of the answer. The answer to procurement's long-standing complaints of low stakeholder buy-in to their procurement process and methodology. And, simultaneously, the answer to stakeholders' pointed question about procurement that drives their low buy-in levels, "But why does it take so long?" Procurement teams performed miracles during the height of the pandemic crisis, and stakeholders liked what they saw – a more responsive procurement process in tune with urgent business needs. Therefore, post-crisis stakeholder demands for a procurement service that is better, faster, cheaper and more responsive may now be overwhelming. Can procurement now leverage this new goodwill and use agile procurement as a tool to make such responsiveness permanent?

This is the key question we have been asking at PASA Agile in Australia and New Zealand. At PASA AGILE, we have now completed numerous LAP workshops both online and offline with Mirko and his extended team.

We have also fulfilled several agile procurement coaching assignments supporting procurement team undertaking agile procurement projects and running their first BIG ROOM supplier engagement workshops at the fulfillment of their agile procurement projects.

Agile procurement works well in theory and in practice, for the right procurement projects, and we at PASA are keen to continue the journey."

–Jonathan Dutton FCIPS I Chief Executive PASA

"John Donne once wrote "no man is an island entire of itself". As the world becomes more complex and interconnected, those words become even more important than they were in 1624. True value can only be created when individuals and organizations come together in a common purpose. And yet, despite this fact, most organizations struggle to build truly collaborative partnerships. Instead, they build fragile relationships on the underlying premise of distrust. But where many see challenge, within this book you will see opportunity. This is your moment to create truly agile partnerships and bring your procurement teams into the 21st century (and perhaps via the 17th for a moment). What agility brings into procurement are the abilities to trust (but check) and inspect (& adapt). Capabilities necessary for organizations to be able to balance governance and risk in order to thrive, together, in the modern economy."

— **Evan Leybourn** Head of Thought-Leadership and Advocacy (co-founder) Business Agility Institute

"I was impressed with Lean-Agile Procurement from the very first time that I saw it. So impressed, in fact, that we wove ideas and strategies from LAP into the Vendor Management portion of Project Management Institute (PMI)'s Disciplined Agile toolkit. If you're involved in procuring anything of material importance for your organization then you need to read this book.„

— **Scott Ambler** Consulting Methodologist, Ambysoft Inc.

"Procurement is the gateway, absolutely the gating factor, to business response. No company can on-board a better supplier or improve a part design in production faster than they can procure. The collaborative, responsible and accelerated procurement methods "Lean-Agile Procurement" described in the book are business tested globally, government accepted, and your accelerator to increase the speed of innovation in your company."

— **Joe Justice** Authored Scrum Master (book), created eXtreme Manufacturing, founded WIKISPEED, lectures on #JoeDX. Tesla alum.

„Culture has been a key impediment to increased agility for over two decades, and yet it continues to elude and frustrate organizational leaders. Corporate governance and finance policies, formed by prior generations, act as protectors of that legacy culture in the name of risk management. The problem is that risks have changed, but the policies and resulting culture haven't. Enter Lean-Agile Procurement, a significant step to bridging this gap and bringing forward one slice of corporate policy and governance into the agile generation. The next generation of corporate winners will be those whose senior financial and governance leaders took this step."
– **Pete Behrens** Founder & CEO, Agile Leadership Journey

"One of the most difficult tasks when it comes to working with a development partner is getting them to build the contract in an Agile way. The way to get to desired results should not be fixed. As the work is done, we will learn along the way and adjust both what will be done and how it will be accomplished. Procurement departments need to start building contracts that allow more flexibility for what is being delivered and how that is accomplished. This enables the people doing the work to act with greater agility. This book provides great direction to help organizations move from a traditional vendor or supplier management approach to a true partner relationship, working together toward a common goal."

— **Eric Naiburg** Chief Operating Officer at Scrum.org

"Procurement can either accelerate and organization or hold it back. Agile procurement practices enable an enterprise to react quickly to changing needs, supply chain challenges, and rapid change. In my experience, procurement is the key enabler of Agile across the entire business."

— **JJ Sutherland** CEO Scrum inc.

"Many people talk about agility; fewer people really understand it; even fewer have internalized it to the point where it guides their thinking and behavior. Mirko Kleiner is one of those people. Agility is about responding to change, managing risk, and activating collective intelligence to get better results, sooner. It's about skipping bureaucracy and focusing on the essentials. It started in software, but today, agility is essential throughout the organization, and indeed, beyond organizational borders. Lean-Agile Procurement introduces a new paradigm to the procurement process. You will likely find yourself rethinking your assumptions as you discover new and better ways of establishing collaboration across company boarders. This book is a must-read for anybody on the client or vendor side of the table in procurement, sourcing, or contracting."

— **Peter B. Stevens** Author, Ten Agile Contracts: Beyond Fixed-Price, Fixed-Scope & Personal Agility: Unlocking Purpose, Alignment, and Transformation

Dedication

First and foremost, I'd like to thank my family and especially my partner Andrea for making all of this possible - you are the love of my life!

Many thanks to Dan Murphy, who helped me improve my Swiss-English and is a real partner in „crime", as well as to all the contributors of case studies, forewords, etc.

I also dedicate this book to all the visionary minds and trailblazers who have tirelessly championed the cause of Lean-Agile Procurement. Your unwavering commitment to redefining traditional paradigms has illuminated a transformative path for the procurement landscape. To the daring souls who dared to challenge the status quo, to the strategists who envisioned a future where collaboration supersedes competition, and to the practitioners who fearlessly embraced change to cultivate more efficient, responsive, and innovative procurement practices.

I look forward to collaborating and challenging the status quo with all my friends, partners, customers and trainers in the global movement of the LAP Alliance.

ISBN

This book could be found in different versions:

- ISBN 978-3-9525909-0-4 PDF
- ISBN 978-3-9525909-2-8 eBook
- ISBN 978-3-9525909-1-1 Hardcopy

Copyright

1. Introduction

In today's rapidly evolving business landscape, organizations are continuously seeking ways to enhance their agility, responsiveness, and adaptability. Lean-Agile Procurement emerges as a transformative approach that revolutionizes the traditional procurement process, enabling businesses to meet the dynamic demands of the market. Combining the principles of Lean and Agile methodologies, Lean-Agile Procurement embodies a customer-centric, iterative, and collaborative approach that redefines strategic procurement and the way vendors are treated.

> „This is a Game Changer!"
> – **Phil Thomas**, Chief Procurement Officer Hargreaves Lansdown (former CPO of Barclays)

Lean-Agile Procurement promotes a fundamental shift from low trust relationships with suppliers to true partnerships where all parties do their best to create a win-win situation. The focus is no longer solely on fixed requirements and long term contracts. Embracing Agile values, Lean-Agile Procurement emphasizes the importance of cultural and social fit to solve today's complex problems together. For this reason, people from all parties, especially all experts who may be involved in the delivery, meet as early as possible to share any risks, assumptions, concerns, etc., and thus improve the initial ideas together across companies.

> *„I've awarded many, many contracts, but I've never been hugged by a supplier at the end of it, when I told him that he won the contract. That tells you something."*
> *— **Serge Kolman**, Procurement & Contracts Manager, Dunedin City Council*

Through this book, we embark on a journey to explore the core principles, patterns, and practices that underpin Lean-Agile Procurement. From reimagining vendor selection to optimizing contract negotiations, we delve into the intricacies of implementing lean-agile principles throughout the procurement lifecycle. Through real-life examples and case studies, we illustrate how organizations from diverse industries have successfully harnessed Lean-Agile Procurement to achieve transformative outcomes. Join us in uncovering the power of Lean-Agile Procurement as a catalyst for innovation, collaboration, and competitive advantage in an ever-evolving business landscape.

Awards

Lean-Agile Procurement has been recognized and awarded by the top three procurement alliances and professional bodies. The winning cases come from both the private and public sectors and different industries.

Table: Awards

Award	Awarded by	Winner
Outstanding Cooperation & Collaboration APAC - Innovation & Excellence Awards 2023	World Commerce & Contracting	Dunedin City Council

Procurement Consultancy Project Award - World Procurement Awards 2020	Procurement Leaders	SwissCasinos Group & flowdays.net
Best Procurement Consultancy Project - Supply Management Awards 2018 Europe	Chartered Institute of Procurement & Supply	CKW Group & flowdays.net

Lean-Agile Procurement Adoption Benefits

When contrasting Lean-Agile Procurement with traditional sourcing methods like RFPs, the differences are striking. RFPs, are characterized by their lengthy documentation, fixed requirements, and prolonged decision-making cycles, can inadvertently stifle innovation and limit organization agility. In other words, today's RFPs are designed and best suited for sourcing with few unknowns. In stark contrast, Lean-Agile Procurement streamlines the process, enabling organizations to swiftly identify changing needs and pivot accordingly. For instance, while an RFP might take several months to reach a vendor selection stage, Lean-Agile Procurement can expedite this process to mere days or weeks, sometimes hours, often with better quality and less risk. This agility not only accelerates time-to-market but also promotes collaboration and creativity throughout the procurement journey.

Table 1: Benefits of adopting LAP

Benefits	Lean-Agile Procurement	Sourcing via RfP
1. Agility	Rapidly adapts to changing requirements and market shifts.	Typically follows a linear and inflexible process.
2. Collaboration	Promotes closer vendor-buyer partnership and creativity.	Often limits collaboration to formalized stages.
3. Incremental Value	Delivers value incrementally, ensuring early benefits.	Often delays value realization until project end.

4. Risk Management	Mitigates risks through continuous monitoring and adjustment.	Relies on upfront risk assessment, which can miss dynamic factors.
5. Time-to-Market	Accelerates time-to-market by 400 to 800% with quicker vendor selection.	Involves longer decision-making cycles and delays.

Beyond speed, the value of Lean-Agile Procurement extends to risk mitigation and cost-effectiveness. Traditional approaches often lock organizations into rigid contracts, leaving little room for adaptation should circumstances change. In Lean-Agile Procurement, the incremental delivery of value enables stakeholders to assess progress continuously and make informed decisions. This iterative nature reduces the risk of costly missteps and ensures that resources are optimally allocated. As a result, Lean-Agile Procurement has demonstrated an average recommendation rate of 9 out of 10 from both the buyer and the supplier. Including the non-winning suppliers.

The following diagram provides a good overview of the value proposition and benefits from the perspective of the 3 key roles involved.

Source: LAP Alliance

Key Roles	Value Proposition	Benefits
Business & other Stakeholders	For **complex business cases** that **require external** support, services, or products LAP offers a **collaborative approach** to **select & deliver** better outcomes faster together	100-800% improved Lead Time via Cross-Capabilities / -Function /-Company Collaboration in avg. 50% less efforts Coping Uncertainty and minimizing Risks via short Feedback-/Delivery cycles up to 80% improved Spent via Outcome-based Approach 9 out of 10 Satisfaction Rate via optimal Stakeholder / Vendor involvement Keeping Driver-Seat from Idea till value delivered (no handovers) Flexible Appraoch that even allows to fall back to a traditional approach if needed

Procurement	For **strategic sourcing cases** that **can't be specified & sourced easily** Lean-Agile Procurement offers a **collaborative approach** to **get involved as early as possible** to source and deliver **better outcomes faster together** with the business & the partner	100-800% improved Lead Time of strategic sourcing cases early involvement at Kickoff of case up to 80% Savings via Outcome-based Approach Coping Uncertainty and minimizing Risks via short Feedback-/Delivery cycles 9 out of 10 Satisfaction Rate across all stakeholder groups Keeping Driver-Seat in terms of Procurement Governance / Process / Policies Incfluence about e.g. supplier landscape

Supplier/s (Sales & Delivery)	For **complex project requests** that **can't be offered easily** Lean-Agile Procurement offers a **collaborative approach** to **sell and deliver better outcomes faster**	Minimized lead time / efforts from request to answer / award via Cross-Company Collaboration via a workshop Freedom how to solve an expected outcome within agreed 'guardrails' Coping Uncertainty and minimizing Risks via early involvement of delivery team even during Sourcing A contract on the same eye-level, that supports agile ways of working in delivery No Penalties, Change Management for small changes and other unnecessary overhead 9 out of 10 Satisfaction Rate between supplier & buyer

In a world where speed is the new currency of business, Lean-Agile Procurement stands as a beacon of innovation, offering benefits that eclipse those of traditional sourcing methodologies. By embracing the principles of adaptability, collaboration, and incremental value delivery, organizations can position themselves at the forefront of their industries, ready to navigate the complexities of a rapidly evolving marketplace with confidence and prowess.

Intended audience for this book

This book is essential reading for business leaders from the buyer- and supply-er side. It also applies across all industry segments including both the private and public sector. If you're interested in transforming procurement, a pioneering change and, or a championing the agility of organizations this book can provide you the information you need to reimagine the future of procurement and usher in an era of adaptive partner ecosystems.

In particular, this book should be of interest to procurement professionals, project managers, supply chain executives, vendor relationship managers, Agile coaches, Lean practitioners, IT leaders, innovation directors, contract managers, and senior executives across industries. It provides actionable insights and real-world strategies to drive innovation, collaboration, and sustainable competitive advantage.

About the author

Mirko Kleiner, a seasoned thought leader and practitioner, initiated a global movement in Lean-Agile Procurement seven years ago. He's also a serial entrepreneur who founded the Lean-Agile Procurement Alliance - The Global Certification Body, yo.blue and co-founded flowdays.net, an agile consultancy in Switzerland and Germany. Through his dynamic leadership, consulting, and speaking engagements, Mirko continues to inspire professionals and organizations worldwide to embrace agility, innovation, and adaptive practices to help them achieve greater impact, faster together.

Disclaimer

While this book offers comprehensive insights into Lean-Agile Procurement practices, it is crucial to recognize that each organizational context is unique. Successful application of these practices demands a nuanced understanding of individual circumstances, industry specifics, and the dynamic interplay of factors. Moreover, the effective implementation of Lean-Agile Procurement hinges on a solid foundation of background knowledge and experience in both Lean and Agile values and principles. Additionally, local laws and regulations play a significant role in shaping the boundaries of procurement strategies, necessitating a careful consideration of legal and compliance aspects. This book aims to provide a guiding framework, but readers are encouraged to exercise discretion and seek professional advice when tailoring these practices to their particular situations.

References and permissions

The contents in this book are extensively referenced to authoritative sources and supported by proper citations. The presented case studies have been included with explicit permission from the organizations, ensuring accurate portrayal and ethical publication.

2. Why does the RfX Process need a major Upgrade?

Image source: awritersden.files.wordpress.com/

The History[1]

Although people have been trading since ancient times, procurement is a relatively new discipline and was unknown before 1800. One of the first mentions is in 1832 in Charles Babage's book On the Economy of Machinery and Manufactures. He points to the need for a 'materials man' in the mining industry to select, purchase and track the goods and services required. There used to be local markets with little competition. Everyone knew each other and would go to the local blacksmith, for example, and order a new pick in person. Products were highly individual and handmade.

The Industrial Revolution cemented the importance of procurement. Marshall Kirkman's 1887 book, The Handling of Railway Supplies - Their Purchase and Disposition, detailed the strategic contributions of procurement to the railway industry, par-

---

[1]   Historie summarized from blog post by Mike Nolan | SourceSuite.com

ticularly in sourcing goods from developed parts of the country and bringing them south and west. In other words, the markets were developing across the country, there were some initial larger players, but there was still little competition. The focus of the industry was on standardization and mass production of simple to complicated products. Suppliers were no longer known personally, so requests for information (RfI) were published in newspapers and suppliers sent their proposals by post. The RfI/RfP process was born (let's call this RfP version 1.0, or RfP 1.0 for short).

Today, in the information age, new technologies are constantly evolving procurement. The digital revolution started in the late 20th century with the internet, email and the web. It continues today with e-procurement solutions, reverse auctions, etc. The underlying goal is to make the tendering process ever more efficient and streamlined (RfP 2.0). This is necessary as markets have become globalized, competition is fierce and customer requirements have become highly complex.

Conclusions

RfP 1.0 was developed in a time before the internet, when buyers and suppliers didn't know each other and direct collaboration was difficult or too expensive. It worked and is still working well for simple and complicated jobs. Because these requirements could be described, understood and estimated by an expert. With RfP 2.0, we are still following the same basic approach as in the 19th century. We have just applied modern, digital tools to it and become more efficient. But complex tenders with a lot of unknown or innovation, for example in IT, still take months and with RfP 2.0 we lose the opportunity for creative solutions and innovation.

Is the sole focus on efficiency enough to cope with the current and future complexity of market and customer requirements?

A Closer Look at the Evidence

Image source: topdreamer.com

Let us take a look at some interesting facts and experiences from the field of handling complex tenders with the classic RfP process.

> „It's funny how hiring practices have changed dramatically over the years, but pitching remains comparatively stagnant"
> — **Avi Dan**, Marketeer & Author at Forbes.-com

In the previous chapter we've learned, that the RfP 1.0 was initially developed at the end of 19th Century and one of its main **purposes** was to **overcome the distance between buyer and supplier**. Furthermore it **worked well for simple to complicated tenders**, where experts who could create exact specifications with little to no unkowns and accurately estimate scope. In this chapter and beyond we will focus to **complex tenders** that leverage RfP2.0. An example of a complex tender would be the evaluation of a new software product and provider for example, or for the service of a new marketing agency.

Just 20% of all features shipped are really used by customer

No matter how we've evaluated and/or built a product or service, it's important to understand that only 20% of all features shipped are often used by our customers. [2].

---

[2]   Standish Group, 2013

Image source: Microsoft.com

Do you e.g. remember this fancy, but useless paper-clip assistant in MS Office?-In other words we are **guessing the useful features during specification** and we are again **guessing / interpretation of these specs while creating an offer.** The distance between buyer and supplier, that was built by the Rf-P2.0, doesn't help here.

Engineers love the solution, this prevents innovation

In software projects we usually have engineers on both sides (buyer/supplier) to support the tender. Engineers love technical solutions, so the specifications often describe the solution (features and functions). In my practice I have seen RFPs with hundreds of lines of functional specifications. No one could tell us who asked for what and why.

"The observer influences the system & the system influences the observer"
– quantum theory

As a result, creativity is stifled and suppliers simply deliver the solution.

KCOM reports in his analyses, that only **30% of RFPs** for consumer-focused projects **required suppliers to explain** how the IT project would **improve the experience for customers**. The remainder focused exclusively on IT metrics[3].

---

[3]   KCOM, a communications and IT services provider, has carried out a detailed examination of RFPs it received over the past 18 months for strategic IT projects. https://www.cips.org/en/supply-management/news/2017/july/it-rfps-have-barely-evolved-in-decades/?

Estimation of a complex Problem doesn't work

The next important thing to consider is that **we are all extremely bad at absolute estimation of a complex problem**. The NASA reported that the absolute estimate of a complex problem can vary by 400% in either direction at an early stage. [4]. Apart from the fact that it's very difficult to give an estimate for the whole solution at an early stage, we should accept that the **scope becomes variable** when solving complex problems. This leaves us with only the cost, time and quality to fix.

> „Costs = f(Time, Quality, ?Scope?)
> **– Mirko Kleiner**

Let me tell you a funny story. Once we received an RfI with only 5-10 rough bullet points. The buyer asked us for a first rough estimate. Based on our experience and expected team size multiplied by time we came up with CHF 1.7 million. When our engineers went through all the detailed specifications of the RfP 2.0, the total estimate was CHF 1.75 million.

---

[4]   Cone of uncertainty, NASA's Software Engineering Lab 1990

The thing is, we've lost another 3 months without adding value to the customer. We were unable to deliver value earlier and may have lost the window of opportunity.

RfP 2.0 are expensive

Executing a complex tender is expensive for both buyer and supplier. I know from my own experience that we've invested, for example, 5-6 FTE's over a period of 2-3 months in complex e-commerce tenders with a spend volume of several million. This equates to an investment of CHF 150-250,000 for a single proposal.

> „Complex tenders e.g. in IT usually takes us 3-6 months and a lot of effort in the procurement as well as in the business"
> — CPO of a German private Bank

In discussions with several CPOs and procurement organizations, we've found that the preparation and execution of a complex RFP requires a similar amount of effort on the buyer's side. The problem is that these costs are often not included in the TCO.

Are you hiring an agency's past or future?

Forbes wrote about the RfP2.0 in context of hiring marketing agencies, that it might give a rough idea of an agency's past accomplishments, and these can inform somewhat of what's ahead. However, we're not hiring an agency's past, we're hiring its future. And that future is more likely to be a reflection of an agency leadership's vision, the people it hires, and their willingness to embrace what's coming rather than preserve what's been. [5]

> „You're hiring for the future, you'd want to know that they are prepared for it."
> — **Avi Dan**, Marketeer & Author at Forbes.-com

We'd want to know if they have a clear sense of the new consumer, and the technologies and platforms that make listening more important than talking. A forward thinking leadership should have a pretty good point of view about how social media, technol-

---

[5]   Forbes.com

ogy, and the migration away from interruptive messages are changing communications.

KCM's report showed, that a fifth (21%) of RFPs were for projects to update restrictive, non-compliant or even failing legacy technology, but **only half** of these **sought innovation** from potential suppliers and **only 17% requested a future-proof proposition** [6].

ESG, Diversity, Circular Economy, .. Procurement can't know it all?

Procurement is faced with a host of new, important issues such as Environmental, Social and Governance (ESG) considerations such as, diversity, circular economy, etc., that need to be incorporated into sourcing. However, with each new issue, the transactional nature of the RfP2.0 pushes the boundaries of what is possible. New roles and teams dealing with e.g. ESG are not integrated into the sourcing process or become additional stakeholders.

---

[6]   KCOM, a communications and IT services provider, has carried out a detailed examination of RFPs it received over the past 18 months for strategic IT projects.

„Just 14% of 5,000 employees across France, Italy, Germany, Spain, and the UK who responded to the survey said they felt confident about making more sustainable purchases on behalf of their business."
−Report by Amazone Business

All this slows down the schedule, increases costs, and most of all adds significant risk. RfP2.0 is just not equipped to deal with these highly complex procurements and many unknowns. The up front planning and requirements definition and rigid scope definition, allow no opportunity for feedback during the process This can be overwhelming for procurement professionals.

RfP2.0, the Vendors Perspective

From my own experience, as a vendor, there is a major investment required, just to participate in the RfP2.0 process, so that we've carefully chosen where to participate. In the majority of cases we declined because the changes of winning didn't merit the investment required to participate. Often there was no opportunity to establish a connection to the customer or any other USP. As such, we have completely avoided Public tenders via RfP2.0, which focus solely on price.

> "Brands are not hiring agencies to create perfect RFP responses that dazzle the brand managers. Rather, brands (should) want to hire an agency that will create unique communications that dazzle audiences. So, judging an agency by its ability to fill out an RFP is testing for the wrong talent. 5)"
> **–Kirk Cheyfitz**, Chief Content Officer Magazine / Content Marketing Agencies

> "We rarely participate in agency-search RFPs. We're against spec pitches but might respond to a request for information about Velocity. Our process depends on a lot of pretty intensive input. Pitches that ask for our ideas based on very little information are unlikely to generate great work. And they take a lot of time and effort that our current clients are essentially paying for. 5)"
> **–Doug Kessler**, Founder, Velocity Partners

If you Google RfP, you'll find many more similar statements. We think it's a shame that a process is holding us back from strong and more innovative partnerships.

Conclusion

RfP2.0 doesn't work for complex tenders or strategic sourcing cases. RfP2.0 provides no mechanism to discover unknowns , so we can't specify the scope without creating waste. In RfP2.0 we spend so much time in the up front planning stage and are still left with unknown unknowns during implementation. In addition, by the time we get to implementations we have consumed more than half the budget and schedule with little value and lots of risk in return. It makes more sense to start discovery early through small iterative implementations to uncover the assumptions, mitigate risks, and validate cost, value. . In complex tenders, we should focus on the needs of the end user/customer and look for a future-proof partner rather than a solution based on current state. This can only happen if we involve the end user, the business and the potential partner in finding a new solution. If the process encourages collaboration and innovation, suppliers may become interested in competing again.

All this leads us to the conclusion that we need a major upgrade of the RfP, the RfP 3.0!

The RfP 3.0 „Request for Participation" - A Major Upgrade, but NO silver Bullet!

Image source: pinimg.com

Let's take a look at RfP 3.0, the Request for Participation, and how it improves the competitive advantage of buyers and suppliers, specifically, in complex procurements.

"Lean-Agile Procurement reduces and distributes risk through incremental and value-added funding for improved business outcomes."
*– **Pete Behrens**, Former Board Member of Scrum Alliance*

In the previous chapters we learned that RfP 2.0 doesn't work with complex tenders. The facts underline what we all assumed. We can't predict or estimate the unknowns, and we can't specify scope without creating waste. We would need so much time to investigate and analyze, that we might as well start iteratively with implementation, gathering real evidence and understanding the underlying assumptions. We've also learnt to focus on the end user/customer's needs, constantly validate them and look for a future-proof partner rather than a predefined solution. If we don't fundamentally reinvent RfP 2.0, we may lose more and more potential partners, and with them the opportunity for unexpected innovation and a potential competitive advantage.

In summary, RfP3.0 is a major upgrade from RfPx, that enables collaboration and innovation. We call it the "Request for Participation". But what does it look like?

The Thing with Trust

Unlike RfP2.0 where the basis for the relationship with the vendor is contractual, in RFP3.0, the relationship is based on true partnership, through trust and transparency. Notice we said **partnership instead of relationship**, that's the first subtle yet significant change with RfP3.0. In an ideal world, we could assume 100% trust by just picking a partner and starting to iteratively explore solutions., RfP3.0, although it doesn't go that far along the trust continuum, it is a major step toward trusting the partner and co-creation of the solution, which is the foundation of the value proposition for RfP3.0. The funny thing about trust is that it works both ways. This is often forgotten. In other words, we need to build trust and reduce risk for both sides (buyer and partner) at the same time. To do this, we can create sophisticated Agile contracts that describe and address collaboration, scope, timing, budget, quality, warranty, etc. Personally, I don't believe in this way and I'm more with Marco Zoppi.

„If the customer is starting to quote from the contract the cooperation has just found it's end"
*—**Marco Zoppi** († 2015), CEO youngculture*

In the 1960s, social psychologist Douglas McGregor developed two contrasting theories [7] that explained what motivates people, and therefore what management style should be applied. He labeled these Theory X and Theory Y. Theory Y assumes people are generally motivated to do their job and need to be enabled, while theory X believes people are basically lazy, unmotivated and need oversight and management to ensure they do their job. Sure, we have to deal with the contractual issues in every procurement, however, I'm a firm believer in (Theory Y), that people should be enabled, versus RfP2.0 which is more on the Theory X side of the continuum that requires oversight and control to achieve its objectives.

---

[7]   Douglas McGregor, Theory X/Y

Instead we should explore lean and Agile cooperation models and contracts, that are fair, foster trust, and enable people by e.g.

- fair risk sharing
- a team-bonus / money for nothing, if we are achieving team goals earlier
- work / fund just stages, with the option of an early exit at any time
- partnering / open books / joint venture / transparency

In this way the partnership stays **adaptive instead of fixed**. In my opinion, that's true Agile contracting, however, that topic is a whole other story, which we will cover in more depth in Chapter 9.3.

Paradigm Changes

Currently Agile is the only approach we know, to deal with complexity, based on its iterative approach of BUILD, MEASURE, LEARN in order to evolve toward intended high value outcome(s)..

In RfP2.0, there is a major assumption, namely, that we can know and list all of the features, functions, specifications, and solutions in advance (**wants**). In complex procurements there are so many unknown unknowns that this assumption is no longer valid, and assuming the solution in advance means that all other innovative options are not even considered. Therefore in RfP3.0 we start with the intended outcome (**needs**), assume very little, co-create with cross-functional teams and base our decisions on evidence collected during the BUILD, MEASURE, LEARN iterative cycle. The solution gets refined through the process driven by value - something the Agile community refers to as "emergent".

A significant departure from RfP2.0 is the cross-functional team that engages in much more direct and interactive communication. It is only with this participative approach that brings a cross-pollination of cognitive diversity that we can bring this creative, innovative solution to procurement. The potential partner and all stakeholders from both sides (business, executives, lawyer, compliance, buyer, customer / user, developer, etc) need to be involved at once, focused on the same outcomes.

And YES, as we do this all together in ONE - BIG Room which allows both sides to communicate, interact and collaborate face to face to ensure such elements as:

- aligning with customer needs
- testing and validating assumptions
- checking if the partner is future proof
- validating cultural fit
- validating technical match (soft-/hard skills), and
- ensuring compliance, etc.

Only with this participative, creative development can we create real innovation and first validations with the stakeholders available and present in the room. Another advantage of this approach is speed and agility. If we get all stakeholders in one BIG ROOM we can make decisions immediately and achieve results in Days instead of Months. We see similar benefits from other examples of this kind of participative governance approach including, Design Thinking, Hackathons, etc.

Acceptance of Uncertainty

But how do we deal with the uncertainty of an "unknown" solution in procurement, when scope becomes variable? LAP is not the only discipline to have dealt with this kind of challenge.

In recent years business strategy planning and development has moved from creating large strategy and planning documents toward a more visual approach. To this end, many organizations have replaced large planning and strategy documents with lighter tools like the Business Model Canvas[8]. The Business Model Canvas is a structured single page describing a business model of an organization, a product, or service. Eric Ries's book "Lean Startup"[9], also leverages the Business Model Canvas, that outlines an Agile approach for early validation of hypotheses that illustrate how to quickly establish a firm and win a customer/market.

---

[8]   Business model canvas, by Alexander Osterwalder
[9]   Lean startup, by Eric Ries

The general advantages of a canvas are:

- it's just one page and we have to focus to what really matters
- it's a good overview / summary, that makes the essence transparent
- it makes things comparable
- it keeps us aware, that everything is connected and influences each other
- it's a tool, that fosters collaboration and communication, and we could use it every day to update our validations with customers /users/team.

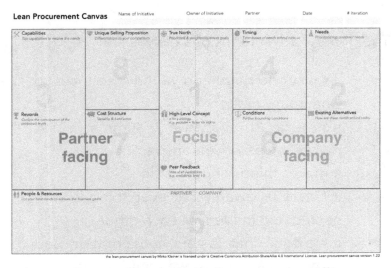

Image Source: Lean-Agile Procurement Alliance

The Lean Procurement Canvas[10], is a modification / adoption of the Business Model Canvas for procurement. It has 3 main areas:

1. **Focus** - Strategic themes / goals (WHY we need this partnership)
2. **Customer facing** - Customer needs, timing, conditions, etc (WHAT we'd like to solve with this partnership)

---

[10] The Lean Procurement Canvas by Mirko Kleiner & LAP Alliance is licensed under a Creative Commons Attribution-ShareAlike 4.0 International License. Lean procurement canvas version 1.24 More under lean-agile-procurement.com

3. **Partner facing** - Capabilities, Unique Selling Propositions (USPs), etc. (HOW we'd might solve the customer needs)

After ideating with the Business Model Canvas, it's very easy to go through the strategy (WHY) and customer needs (WHAT) and add the timing (WHEN), people (WHO) and conditions (WHEREIN) in a matter of hours. This gives us the basic information to start a participative event with one or more potential partners. In this joint event we work out what is valuable for us to decide to start an adaptive partnership. This could be working out together more concrete customer needs and appropriate solutions, an Agile roadmap of the next stage, etc. Basically, we complete The Lean Procurement Canvas together and decide.

Start early, validate often

What applies to a business model and, more specifically, to customer needs, also applies to a partnership. Instead of wasting time on non-valuable work, we start as early as possible and constantly validate the joint achievements step by step, thus validating the partnership. In this way, the lean procurement canvas becomes the tool for managing your evolving **Adaptive Partner Ecosystem**[11].

It turns out that the Lean Procurement Canvas can be applied to all industries that need to manage complex tenders, adaptive partnerships, etc. Besides the business benefits, what's most important for us,, is that with the participative approach of RfP3.0, and the trust it develops encourages an atmosphere of **FUN** in the faces of all stakeholders!

RfP3.0 is no Silver Bullet

Just to be clear, the RfP3.0 is NOT intended to replace the RfP2.0. It's a new complementary tool in your procurement toolbox for complex and particularly strategic sourcing cases, while the RfP2.0 remains the right tool for commodity, and complicated sourcing cases, where subject matter experts can answer the few unknowns.

---

[11]   Source: LAP Alliance

Lean / Agile - WTF 😵💧☠🙎

Traditional sourcing approaches are still valid, just know where to apply it!

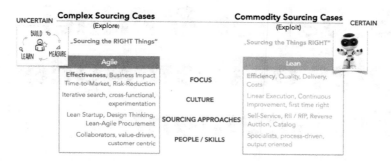

Image source: LAP Alliance

3. Values & Principles of Lean-Agile Procurement

Lean-Agile Procurement is underpinned by a set of core values and principles that redefine the traditional procurement landscape. At its heart is a commitment to fostering agility, collaboration, and value-driven outcomes. The approach recognizes that the dynamic and rapidly changing business environment demands a departure from rigid, linear procurement processes. Instead, it embraces flexibility, iterative progress, and a deep-seated respect for the needs of all stakeholders involved.

"To solve complex problems a cultural- & social fit is key"
— **Mirko Kleiner**

Our Mission[1]

Similar to the Agile Manifesto [2], we came up with a more sticky mission statement with our 5 pair values. We are uncovering better ways of aligning procurement with agile collaboration by doing it and helping others to do it. Through our work we have come to value:

Table 2: Mission of LAP

DAYS	*instead of*	**MONTHS**
NEEDS	*instead of*	**WANTS**
ADAPTIVE	*instead of*	**FIXED**
PARTNERSHIP	*instead of*	**RELATIONSHIP**
FUN	*instead of*	**PAIN**

That is, while each element on the right is important, we find that emphasizing the elements on the left generally leads to better results.

---

[1]   https://www.lean-agile-procurement.com/mission
[2]   aglimanifesto.org

DAYS instead of MONTHS

In a fast-changing world, time-to-market is one of the key metrics. LAP's approach promises to be fast. It challenges all existing rules & regulations to achieve maximum time-to-market.

> *"Speed is the new Currency of Business"*
> *– **Marc Benioff**, Founder and CEO of Salesforce*

This also includes the principle of incremental value delivery. The approach champions the practice of breaking down huge sourcing projects into smaller, manageable increments, delivering most promising hypotheses and its tangible value first. This not only ensures that value is realized early and consistently, but it also enables the flexibility to adapt and adjust as new information emerges. By embracing experimentation and learning, Lean-Agile Procurement fosters a culture of continuous improvement, where lessons from each iteration inform and enhance subsequent cycles.

NEEDS instead of WANTS

Central to the values of Lean-Agile Procurement is the principle of customer-centricity. This entails actively engaging with both internal customers and external vendors to co-create solutions that align with the ever-evolving requirements of the market. Requirements in a sense of a joint understanding about the customer/user needs. We don't want to just look for features and functions (wants), but surprise the customer/user by delivering business value earlier, with as little waste as possible, while providing room for unexpected evolutions and innovations. If we succeed earlier and stop or pause partnership we celebrate our success and do not continue with non-valuable nice-to-haves ('Wants')!-On the other hand we also respect the needs of the people, who will work together to deliver the solutions.

ADAPTIVE instead of FIXED

To cope with the complexity of strategic sourcing cases we accept uncertainty and don't fix the scope (at least in the area's of the sourcing case where we have unknowns). We keep it flexible and adapt from sourcing to delivery. Additional, we maintain a clear focus of always delivering best value for money. We solve customer/user needs, learn and adapt with each iteration/Sprint. In other words, we do not stick to initial plans and may not stick with initial partners. The evaluation approach dictates partner selection. If another partner is more valuable, we switch. We always define and measure success in terms of business value and make this transparent to everyone involved.

PARTNERSHIP instead of RELATIONSHIP

Changing partners is never considered a loss, rather, the partner interaction is always considered a learning. If we had good experiences within the partnership we may leverage that in the future. We always look for sustainability in partnerships, in conjunction with adaptability. We definitely don't view the customer/vendor relationship as a win-lose, where one wins and the other loses. Instead the intent is to establish true partnerships, where we all meet at the same eye-level.

FUN instead of PAIN

Looking for a new partner and working together as a team should be first of all fun for all participants. We always prefer honest and transparent collaboration, over painful win:lose negotiations. These collaborations are always held between the people, that will potentially work together in the future, therefore, it is critical to ensure strong trust, business, cultural and social fit.

Beware Culture Clashes

Introducing lean-agile principles into traditional procurement organizations can give rise to potential culture clashes as these two paradigms inherently differ in their values and approaches.

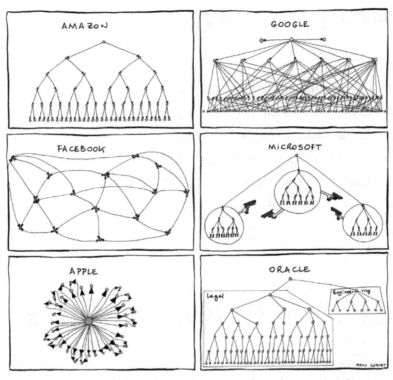

Corporate Culture Map by www.bonkersworld.net

The shift from a linear, process-heavy structure to an adaptive, iterative one can create tension among employees accustomed to well-defined, sequential procedures.

"Culture eats strategy for Breakfast"
– Peter Drucker

The emphasis on collaboration, open communication, and cross-functional teams may challenge hier-

archical decision-making prevalent in traditional set-
tings, leading to resistance and discomfort. Moreover, the concept of embracing change as a constant
can clash with a risk-averse culture that values stabili-
ty and cautious decision-making. Navigating these
clashes requires a careful balance between honoring
established practices and cultivating a mindset that
welcomes agility, innovation, and customer-centricity.

4. The Lean Procurement Canvas

In the previous chapter we only touched on the Lean Procurement Canvas. Let's take a deeper dive into this main Lean Agile Procurement tool. In this chapter you will learn how, when and under what circumstances you can use it. We will also touch on common pitfalls, answer some of the challenges mentioned in the chapter „A Closer Look at the Evidence" regarding RfP2.0 and learn why we think the Lean Procurement Canvas is the most lean Agile contract and risk mitigation framework at the same time!

Where to start & what do all the sections mean?

The Lean Procurement Canvas is a living document that is collaboratively updated by the cross-functional team throughout the product lifecycle. It was originally designed to solve the problem of complex strategic sourcing cases, but it can have a much brought application including a partner management tool!

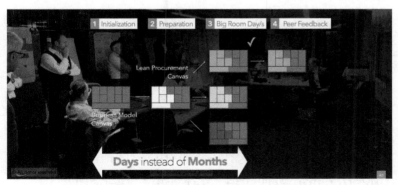

Image Source: LAP Alliance - The Canvas as Partner Lifecycle Management Tool

More about that in a later chapter.

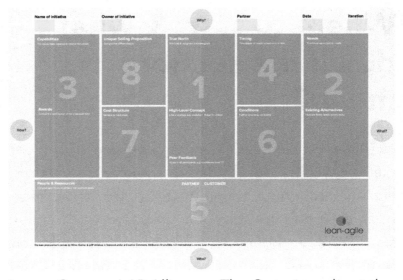

Image Source: LAP Alliance - The Overview about the Lean Procurement Canvas

The Lean Procurement Canvas is divided in 2 main areas:

1. Green / right-hand side: The buyer or customer
2. Blue / left-hand side: The partner or vendor

The starting point is WHY, which both the Green (buyer/customer) side and Blue (vendor/partner) side share. To be truly customer centric, we need to understand the purpose / vision of the customer (High Level Concept). This could be the buyer's whole organization, just a product unit/department or even a team.

True North
Prioritized & weighted business goals

ater?

What are the current strategic goals?
Do we know the priorities?
What is the relative weight of each
strategic goal?
Which goals is this initiative
contributing to?
What are the goals of this partnership?

TIPP: Define your goals impact-based
(Keep ESG, Circular Economy, etc. in
mind)

 ## High-Level Concept
x for y analogy,
e.g. youtube = flicker for videos

What is the vision of each company?
Do we have a match?

,

Image Source: LAP Alliance - True North & High Level
Concept

To do this, we initially start by filling in the Green (buyer/customer) side to establish the High-Level Concept and True North sections together with the key stakeholders requesting this sourcing case. In the True North we define the expected business outcomes and objectives. This is also a good opportunity to cover current global topics like ESG / Sustainability etc.

Timing

ls

?

p?

ːd

ːn

Time-boxes of needs solved now, or later

Does a strategic goal determine a time box?
What needs will be resolved in which Timebox?
Which needs will be done now, what later?
Do we still have all capabilities required?

TIPP: Use your Agile Roadmap to forecast availabilities of 3rd tier supply, cost ceilings, etc.

Conditions

Further bounding conditions

What are our values & principles?
What is our collaboration model?
Do we have open books, fixed margins?
What's the context of this partnership?
Is there a budget cap?
Are we looking for in/outsourcing, short-long-term partnership?
Where will the joint team work?
What's the prior language?
What are the general terms & conditions?

Image Source: LAP Alliance - Timing & Conditions

Together with the True North, the Conditions estab-lish the guard-rails of the product / service to be de-livered in the partnership are often shared, but also the schedule (updated in the Timing section), includ-ing important milestones. An example of a guard rail could be a financial condition such as a budget cap, or a legal condition such as certain standards, rules & regulations, etc.

 ## Existing Alternatives
How are these needs solved today

How do we solve their needs today?
Who are other potential partners?
ns? **What are other potential solutions?**
)? **What happens if we do nothing?**

Image Source: LAP Alliance - Existing Alternatives

Next the Existing Alternatives section is designed to move the discussion beyond a long list of potential partners. Here, powerful questions are posed, such as „what if we don't do it?", „what if we do it our-selves?", „Are there other possible solutions?", etc. The idea is to broaden the horizon of options before zooming in again. This is a good time to ask if the key stakeholders/sponsors if they already have a favorite, and if so, should we still consider other vendors?

The importance of collective intelligence can't be overstated. To deal with the uncertainty and complexity of strategic sourcing cases, we need to leverage, to the greatest extend possible, the experience and knowledge and cognitive diversity of the group/team. First internally, and later with potential partners, and at a later stage, this alignment needs to be revisited.

The numbers on the Lean Procurement Canvas indicate the sequence of progression, through the canvas, or more abstractly:

From WHY -to WHAT -over to HOW, while LAP adds a new dimension WHO

Having the True North, Conditions, and Timing roughly defined enables us to better initially determine the Buyer side's cross-functional team, or the WHO / People & Resources.

Image Source: LAP Alliance - People & Resources

The Buyer side cross-functional and cross-capability team creates with the end-users/customers the WHAT/Customer needs, etc.

 Needs

Prioritised top customer needs

ne

1

**Who are our customers?
What are their behaviors & needs?
Is one of those needs a strategic usp, if yes, do we really want to outsource it?
Are the needs balanced with the weighted strategic goals?**

Image Source: LAP Alliance - Needs

In general, the left-hand side of the canvas is left open to be filled out by the shortlisted vendor(s). However, in the early stage we may have options to add Capabilities / USP / etc. that are important to achieving our outcomes.

75

In the Awards section it's important to note that contrary to a traditional tender, the buyer is looking for more than a list of customer references. LAP is designed to discover the deeper contribution of the people and team proposed by the vendor, and specifically, their successes as a team. For example, if a vendor proposes a team that has been successfully collaborating in other engagements we might expect a lower learning curve.

 Awards

Outline the contribution of the proposed team

What is the contribution of the people who will work together?
Which other customers has this team delighted?
Could we ask person/s from 1st hands?
Has the team contributed in their community?

TIPP: Track partners performance e.g. via Peer Feedback

Image Source: LAP Alliance - Awards

To summarize, the table below outlines the intent of each section of the LAP canvas.

Table: Intent of each section of the canvas

Section of the canvas	Intent
High Level Concept (1)	people need to understand the purpose/vision of their company and of the partner
True North (1)	for an optimal alignment people need a direction
Peer Feedback (1)	transparency about a gut feeling for this cooperation to identify risks continuously
Needs (2)	setting the initial focus to the market instead of the solution
Existing Alternatives (2)	open the focus to any solution possible
Capabilities (3)	check potential solutions/products/etc for the given customer needs
Awards (3)	get an idea of the contribution of the proposed team

Timing (4)	setting fixed timeboxes on a high level so that approaches and forecasts could be compared
People & Resources (5)	getting aware of the people & resources needed to achieve the business goals
Conditions (6)	frame conditions of the agile team
Cost Structure (7)	with a predefined cost structure and pricing model the offers get comparable
Unique Selling Proposition (8)	understand other capabilities and differentiators of the partner

Use the QR-Code below to download The Lean Procurement Canvas in different languages.

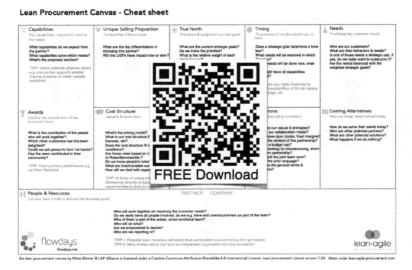

Image Source: LAP Alliance - Free download of Cheat sheet

To make a long story short, The Lean Procurement Canvas covers all topics that are relevant for a contract.

„The Lean Procurement Canvas is the most lean Agile Contract beside a verbal agreement"

*– **Ursula Sury**, Lawyer lic. iur, Vice Director Lucerne University of Applied Sciences & Arts*

The purpose of the canvas is to co-create the contract with all parties involved.

Is one Page really enough for e.g. a $ 1 bn Sourcing Case?

Obviously not, however, similar to the Business Model Canvas it is a nice summary that shows the dependencies between the sections. It is, however, important to note that depending on the context of the case, there are a significant variety and volume of attachments.

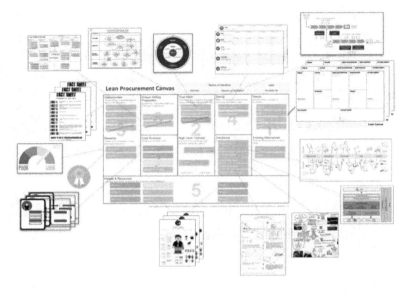

Image Source: LAP Alliance - Attachments to the canvas

Attention: All of the attachments are living documents or hypothesis!

The Canvas a Risk Mitigation Framework

The Lean Procurement Canvas not only revolutionizes procurement practices but also functions as a robust risk mitigation framework. By offering a visual and structured approach, the canvas enables organizations to proactively identify, assess, and mitigate risks inherent in procurement processes. Its systematic layout empowers teams to collaboratively address potential disruptions, fostering a culture of risk awareness and resilience while ensuring smoother and more successful procurement outcomes.

The canvas mitigates 4 key areas of risk:

Business or Partner Risk

If the WHY and WHAT sections of the canvas do not match the proposed solutions / products / services (HOW) of the vendor/partner, this indicates that we don't really have a valid solution and this is not the right vendor/partner.

Partner Risk - Do we have the right partner?

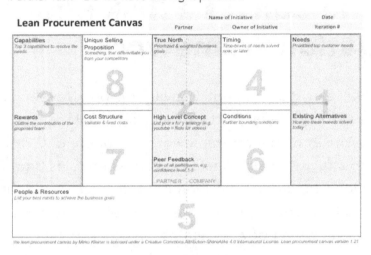

Image source: Lap Alliance - Partner risk

Condition Risk

A strong fit on cultural, technical, legal and non-functional conditions would indicate a strong potential vendor/partner fit, whereas, weak alignment on these areas would suggest a poor partner alignment.

Condition Risks - Is the cost structure of the partner ok?

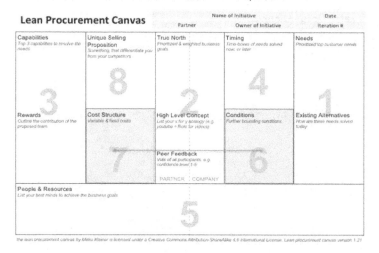

Image source: Lap Alliance - Conditions risk

People Risk

The LAP process enables us to get to know the people we will be working with through its participatory nature. The canvas provides a place to capture those experiences and in LAP this is part of the evaluation criteria. If we don't like the people we might be working with, both in delivery and leadership, then we may be engaging with the wrong vendor/partner.

People Risk - Do we have a good mix of soft- and hard skills?

Image source: Lap Alliance - People risk

Future Risk

If the partner is a perfect fit now, but shows no potential for our future ambitions, then perhaps this is not the best vendor/partner.

Future Risk - Has the partner the potential for the future as well?

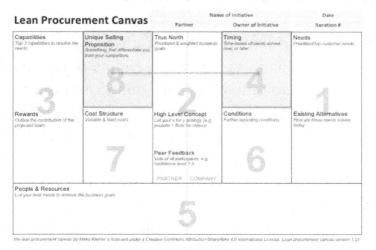

Image source: Lap Alliance - Future risk

In LAP, the cross-functional team monitors all these risks iteratively. At least every time it's updated. Sometimes this is during the shortlisting process, sometimes it is during the contact with the shortlisted suppliers, and sometimes it happens that we have to exclude a supplier even during the workshop in the big room.

The canvas helps to keep track of these risks.

Common Pitfalls

While Lean-Agile Procurement offers a transformative approach, it's essential to navigate potential pitfalls that could potentially arise during its implementation. One common challenge is the clash of the organizational culture with the adaptive culture introduced by LAP. Often the shift towards agility, from established norms, encounters resistance. Additionally, misalignment between procurement and vendor/partner expectations can also lead to difficulties in collaboration, hindering the seamless flow of value. The chart below lists some common potential constraints when implementing LAP.

Table: Lean-Agile Alliance - Pitfalls applying The Lean Procurement Canvas

Pitfall	Better do instead
Create the canvas on your own	The canvas shall be created / updated / reviewed together with the cross-functional team and stakeholders / vendors / end-users/-customers
Create the canvas just once at the beginning	The canvas is a living document that is created initially and evolves over time
The Business is not involved	LAP requires that the business is in lead of the sourcing case and nominates a product owner
Write deliverables in True north and / or in Customer needs	The business objectives as well as the Customer needs shall be outcome-based
Have a favorite but still do multi-vendor sourcing	This is waste, just go for the favorite in a first iteration
Make it too perfect / scientific	Often we put no efforts in look-n-feel and just use sticky notes on the canvas

Too much / detailed attachments	Just create enough information up front so that the vendors get aligned and could commit to a first phase
Assign people	We rather recommend to let the people of the cross-functional team self-select based on needed capabilities
Cross-functional team is incomplete	We don't start the sourcing case until we have all key capabilities in the team with more than 2 days a week availability
Cross-functional team is just responsible for sourcing	To prevent unwanted handovers it's required that key team members are involved in delivery too

Vigilant attention to these pitfalls is crucial to harnessing the full potential of Lean-Agile Procurement.

Application Areas for the Canvas

Although the Lean Procurement Canvas was initially designed to improve strategic sourcing, it can be applied to a multitude of application areas within the procurement landscape. It can and has been used as a strategic guide for reimagining the vendor selection processes, optimizing contract negotiations, and enhancing supplier relationships. Beyond procurement, the canvas extends its utility to areas such as risk management, fostering innovation, and aligning cross-functional teams, becoming an indispensable tool for organizations seeking to infuse Lean principles into their procurement strategies and beyond.

The following is a summary of currently known and applied uses for the Procurement Canvas:

- **Sourcing** - The Canvas optimizes the entire supplier selection process from idea to contract and takes it to a new level.
- **Account Management Tool for Strategic Partners** - After sourcing the Canvas has been seamlessly used as an account management tool - both on the buyer and supplier side - to monitor and plan the partnership more effectively in an iterative way on a single page.
- **Assessment of an existing partnership** - Although most procurement organizations have supplier management tools in place, they often lose sight of the big picture. The Canvas offers the ability to quickly (<1 hour) assess an existing partnership with all the benefits of leveraging diversity by involving all relevant people.
- **Modeling a Partnership's Should State** - Sometimes an existing partnership develops in the wrong direction. The Canvas can help to model the "should state" of the partnership collaboratively, with all the

internal and external people in less than an hour.

- **1 Page Proposal** - Vendors have been inspired by the power of LAP and have started to use it in reverse. The canvas is an effective tool for an initial proposal, but also as a tool for a validation workshop with all key stakeholders. We usually have the ambition to close a deal in less than 1 hour!

- **1 Page Contract** - As we've learnt, the canvas covers all the information needed for a contractual framework. Startups or more disruptive companies started to use the canvas as an Agile contract, skipping the translation into further legal documents.

However you use the Canvas, remember that it's never about the tool, it's always about the conversations, communications and alignment that we create with it!

5. Lean-Agile Procurement - A Framework or a new Mindset?

Ever since I was a software vendor 20 years ago, I've been aware of the fact that the RfP2.0 is somehow the wrong tool for the wrong job. At the time, I observed that customers couldn't articulate what they wanted until they saw it. Seven years ago, when we started to rethink strategic procurement, we realized that it was a lose-lose situation and that we needed a major upgrade that was designed from the ground up. So we started with the powerful question:

„What if we'd only have one day to procure?

Image source: finepowertools.com

That simple question was the germination point for LAP. The whole movement was born out of that question and it's about to become the global standard. Seven years ago we talked about LAP as a new approach, later when people asked us "where are the checklists?" - we called it more of a framework. Today, I'm convinced that LAP is a new way of thinking about procurement!

The thing about complexity and uncertainty is that there's no one approach or framework that fits all. Every sourcing case is different, every company is different, the circumstances and context are different, ...

Repeatedly, LAP seeks to overcome the following key challenges in strategic sourcing:

- **Misalignment / misunderstanding** (internally and externally) due to focus on paperwork and documentation
- **Transactional nature of RfP2.0** including hand-offs between departments where often different people are responsible for sourcing than those for delivery
- **Complexity/unknowns** where requirements are more hypothetical, and often change. Subject matter experts need to be involved as procurement can't make the assumption to know of the details up front and understand it all anymore, e.g. on issues like ESG, AI
- **Long lead times**, which in turn lead to expensive and time consuming change requests in delivery, because the world has changed in the interim.

So what's the alternative, because the Lean-Agile values & principles may not be enough, especially for inexperienced people. Well, over the last 7 years we've identified common challenges and patterns, and how to overcome them.

Please note: Generally speaking LAP is not pre-scriptive. It is not a step-by-step specific process or framework, rather it's more about how to apply good practice to recognize patterns, and how to overcome the most common challenges in strategic sourcing cases.

Image Source: LAP Alliance - The 5 patterns („Steps")
of LAP

Those patterns are summarized in 5 iterative topics (some might call them „steps").

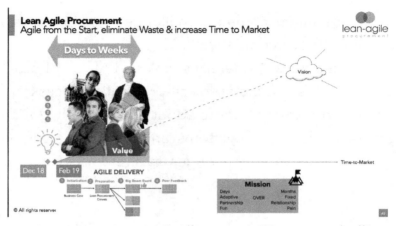

Image source: LAP Alliance - LAP in a nutshell

The visualization above may help you understand how LAP delivers value to the market/customer. At its core is the cross-functional Agile delivery team that's also responsible for sourcing. Depending on the strategic sourcing case, the skills on the team may vary, but the business owner is always leading the team and procurement is a team member that facilitates through the 7-8 sourcing steps. In our experience, the mere fact of having all the skills in place improves time-to-market by 100%! - Using LAP with Scrum[1] as the operating model for the team has shown to improve time-to-market by up to 800%!

---

[1]   https://scrumguides.org

We'll dive into the 5 patterns in a moment. First, let's look at procurement from a different angle.

Procurement is the Investor for the Company / the Government!

"Procurement as the investor for the company/government" encapsulates a profound paradigm shift in the role of procurement. Beyond a transactional function, procurement assumes the role of a strategic investor, shaping the organization's future through supplier partnerships and value creation. By leveraging procurement's influence, organizations can drive innovation, optimize costs, and strategically allocate resources, thereby maximizing their potential for long term growth, success and adaption.

I was shocked to learn years ago that commercial roles such as procurement / sales / etc. are responsible for up to ..

.. **80% of turnover** [2] (in the private sector), and up to ..

.. **15% of GDP** [3] (in the public sector / government)

This made me realize the importance of improving these commercial functions and the direct, positive and powerful impact they have on the business. In more recent times procurement is becoming much more significant and strategic in its impact on the environment and society!

---

[2]   Statistics by CIPS.org
[3]   Statistics by the World Trade Organization

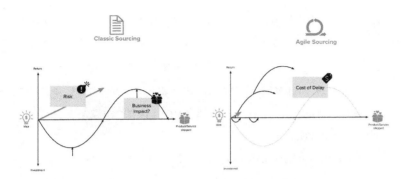

Image source: LAP Alliance - Investors point of view

Let's imagine for a moment that our strategic sourcing case is worth $100 million. The case shown on the left visualization "classic sourcing" RfP2.0, shows a scenario where we'd spend all our investment up front, accumulating massive risk. By contrast, with LAP we accept the uncertainty of a strategic sourcing case. We assume a similar investment strategy as an Angel Investor in a startup and invest in increments to test and validate early and mitigate risk. Perhaps an initial investment of $ 1 million to try to achieve the most valuable hypotheses first so that we're getting hopefully our return as early as possible.

In LAP we apply this principle of incremental funding to sourcing. In the case studies section, you'll learn how we sourced an ERP system in just 2 days. This wouldn't be possible if we had gone for the whole scope at once. We focused on 3 business objectives first, keeping the vision and subsequent objectives in mind, while sourcing only for those 3 in the first stage. This way we still have risks, but they are already significantly minimized. If we use Scrum, the risk window is reduced even further to a week / sprint timeframe.

"Speed is the new currency". If this becomes our mantra, then price negotiations will become less important than they are today. By contrast, price is the key differentiator for commodity products. In LAP it's not unusual to see the buyer side choose a more expensive vendor/partner they can trust to deliver returns sooner. Again, an earlier return or improved time-to-market could mean millions in efficiencies, and significant competitive advantage.

Scaling LAP

LAP works also for small procurements. It scales well with the size of the business case / spend-budgets. Recently a customer with a $ 100,000 business case raised a concern regarding the overhead costs associated with LAP. I responded with the question, „what are the maximum acceptable overhead costs?" The customer responded that the overhead costs should not exceed 10%. As a result, the cross-functional team was given the task of finding a sourcing strategy within an overhead cost budget of $ 10,000, which is equal to 2-3 days internal costs!

The reverse is also true. Large investments, such as a whole new factory or supply chain, can be sliced into different 'product' teams. We used this approach successfully with Lightyear[4], a Dutch scale-up bringing the first solar-powered electric car to market. The body-in-white system team, the skeleton of the car, took end-to-end responsibility for the system, including the required partner ecosystem for design, manufacturing, etc.

---

[4]   https://lightyear.one

A Deeper Dive into the LAP Patterns („Steps")

Initialization

The Initialization in Lean-Agile Procurement serves as the foundation for establishing a successful partnership. It involves assembling the cross-functional team, aligning stakeholders, and establishing a shared vision, setting the stage for an adaptive and collaborative procurement. Vision in the sense of the product/service we are going to develop/improve/launch together with our partner.

Please note: At this stage, the suppliers are usually not yet involved.

The following table gives some insight into the challenge we are trying to solve and the purpose of this pattern:

Table: Lean-Agile Procurement - Initialization

Pattern	Description
Challenge	Because of the functional organization and the transactional nature of the RfP2.0 Strategic Sourcing Cases often lack internal alignment especially between the leadership team and the people on the ground executing the sourcing case
PURPOSE of Pattern	The Buyer side is internally aligned with the strategic aspects of the sourcing case, the sourcing strategy is agreed to, a cross-functional team is setup and empowered
Input	- Business Case is available and has a strategic priority to the organization - Key stakeholders & potential team members are identified and invited to a 1-8 hour (s) kickoff workshop - kickoff workshop is organized

Key activity	1-8 hour/s kickoff-workshop
Output	- Agreed upon co-created outcome, key metrics, conditions and timing - Key capabilities & people are identified for the cross-functional team and beyond - Sourcing strategy & agile collaboration model is defined - Any concerns, risks, etc. are made transparent - Roles are defined & cross-functional team is empowered - Rough timing & next steps are defined
Key Difference to RfP2.0	During initialization we're NOT setting up an agile sourcing team, but an Agile Delivery Team responsible for any partnerships and so for sourcing in a first place too

One of the key differentiators of LAP is that it applies Agile behaviors and principals. Key among these is fact to face meetings. Whenever possible, we meet face-to-face to establish personal contact, to develop trust and collaboration among teams that were most likely stovepiped in the past. This is often the first time people from different departments meet.

Just by bringing the right people together, for 1 hour, we were able to solve a strategic sourcing case with the state of Zurich, Switzerland. The IT department realized that the expected results could be achieved within their existing systems in a matter of weeks, rather than through a massive investment. I'd call that a new record in public procurement!

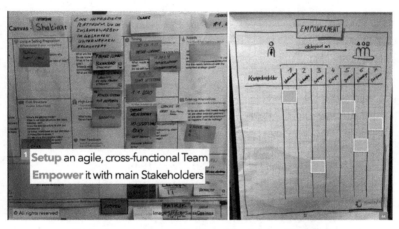

Image source: Swiss Casinos Group

The changes for success increase exponentially when we have cross-departmental alignment on the outcome (True North), strategic guardrails (Conditions), cross-functional team members including decision-making competencies, and next steps / key milestones (Timing). As you can see in the photo, the canvas helps us to guide the deep conversations required to co-create a common alignment.

In the ERP case, the CTO mentioned that the company had a Microsoft/cloud strategy, which we immediately added to the Conditions section of the canvas. This immediately reduced the long list of vendors, allowing the team to focus on what the Microsoft universe had to offer. In this case, we also talked about a 'no customizing' policy. In other words, the company prioritized time-to-market over customer needs and would rather adapt their business processes than customize the software.

The clear defined outcome and timing, enabled the participants of the kickoff to identify and focus on the key skills needed for the Agile delivery team. In addition, we let the current people self-select into the identified roles and/or nominate others. As a golden rule, we only start when all key people are available at least 2 days per week. The product owner should be available at least 4 days per week. This often leads to a portfolio issue, which the current leadership must address immediately.

Please note: The more focused the Agile delivery team is, the faster they can deliver.

Once the team is set up and aligned, the real work begins.

Preparation

Preparation in Lean-Agile Procurement is all about getting ready to meet the shortlisted vendors to co-create their proposals, etc. Sometimes just an hour is needed, sometimes several days or even weeks. Here the team is applying the traditional 7-8 sourcing steps.

> *With LAP we are always compliant within given rules & regulations!*
> *– Mirko Kleiner*

In other words having somebody from procurement on the team, sometimes somebody from compliance, if regulations are affected even the regulator are we always compliant within given rules and regulations!

Only difference is that we're working as a Scrum team with all skills needed at hand. That's why LAP is so efficient, even in government.

The following table gives some insight into the challenge we are trying to solve and the purpose of this pattern:

Table: Lean-Agile Procurement - Preparation

Pattern	Description
Challenge	Because of the functional organization and the service oriented nature of the RfP2.0 the creation of the relevant informations and documentation, especially related to detailed requirements / specification related to Strategic Sourcing Cases is exhausting, time consuming, risks and expensive.
PURPOSE of Pattern	The Agile (cross-functional) delivery team has all key skills to execute the 7-8 sourcing steps as an integrated and independent team

Input	- Business Case
	- Empowered business-led Agile Delivery team
	- Strategic guidance by the key stakeholders / leadership based on the Canvas with key criteria and data points such as True North, Conditions, Timing, etc.
	- Product & impediment Backlog with next tasks and risks
Key activity	- Applying the 7-8 sourcing steps as a Scrum team
	- Gathering e.g. customer needs, directly from the end-users/-customers via e-g- a design thinking workshop
	- Creating a long-/shortlist of potential partners incl. selection criteria and invitation, briefing of shortlisted vendors
	- Preparation an integrated buyer-vendor/partner workshop (The Big Room Workshop) and all needed artifacts such as a draft of an Agile contract framework

Output	- shortlist of potential partners invited - Big Room workshop prepared - draft of an Agile contract framework ready
Key Difference to RfP2.0	The preparation is a team effort and as customer centric as possible. We always prefer to speak with end-users/-customers versus man in the middle

What is true for Initialization is also true for Preparation, and whenever possible we like to get in touch with the end user/customer. This is true customer centricity. It's about listening to individual needs, concerns and questions, and putting them into the context of the sourcing case objectives and guardrails.

Gather **Needs** with **real Users**
Prepare for **Big Room Evaluation Workshop**

Image source: CKW AG

It's a good idea to invite several representatives from each key stakeholder groups, all at the same time, to gather and prioritize their needs. In the photo above with CKW, a government-owned energy company, we invited about 40 people from 9 stakeholder groups to a 4-hour workshop. We explained the sourcing case to them on the spot, using the information on the canvas, rather than wasting our time with glossy PowerPoint slides.

Such a workshop is very effective because we get all the information we need and more at once, we can ask all the relevant questions while updating the different stakeholders at the same time. We have also found that there is a cross-pollination of ideas and innovation from one stakeholder group to another.

It is important to say that according to the definition of Scrum the Product Owner, Business Owner of the Agile Delivery Team is the only authority that prioritizes all these inputs. In this workshop we also take the opportunity to explain the sourcing approach (LAP) and the roles and decision competences. As a result, the team is much more accepted internally.

Please note: LAP doesn't prescribe the agenda or practices used in such a workshop. We've made very good use of various practices depending on the context of the initiative e.g. with User Story Mapping[5] in other occasions we've applied practices from Design Thinking [6], etc.

Imagine having a wall of prioritized sticky notes for each stakeholder group. Simple questions like "what are the absolute must have capabilities", determines our minimum viable product (MvP). The MvP enables the team to focus on the key value in procurement case and in our experience, the elimination of all the „nice to haves" with a focus on essential capabilities, has shown savings of up to 80%!

This combination of focused needs, the traditional sourcing steps, and the canvas, provide a

---

[5]   User Story Mapping by Jeff Patton
[6]   Design Thinking by Larry Leifer, David Kelley &Terry Winograd Stanford University

roadmap to capture all the critical information required for a successful strategic sourcing effort.

If it's a technical solution, we might create an architecture overview including interface descriptions of how this new solution needs to be integrated. We can then use this information to streamline the selection criteria, and the long list of potential partners, resulting in a much more efficient approach. Additional needs analysis and sequencing is a team effort. These items can be placed in the Backlog Items in our Product Backlog [7] to be implemented in increments over time, as determined by the team. At the end of each Sprint [8] we review the Backlog Items that have been completed with our key stakeholders and the end user/customer. This continues to keep the focus on value creation, while minimizing the risk of making mistakes, not only in the preparation, but throughout the agile delivery.

Unlike an RfP2.0, we will share just enough information with shortlisted suppliers to confirm that they are capable and interested in participating in the Execution / Big Room Workshop.

---

[7]   https://scrumguides.org
[8]   https://scrumguides.org

Guiding question: What do we want to achieve and test with the vendors we've invited?

The biggest task in LAP is to organize the Big Room Workshop (in person or virtually). The guiding question for this task is what do we want to achieve and test with the vendors we've invited? The intent of the Big Room Workshop is to award and sign a contract with one or more vendors. The second part of the guiding question is even more important, what do we want to test? By having the vendors present, including key people from a potential delivery team, we can assess all aspects of a potential solution such as technology, current challenges and how they'd solve them, etc?

In summary, during Preparation, we prepare everything needed to co-create the proposals with the potential partners in the Big Room Workshop.

Please note: It's recommended to start immediately with the preparation of the specific legal framework based on Agile values & principles (also called an „Agile Contract"). As this will be new to most lawyers, additional time will be needed, hence the early start.

If it's not possible to have just use the canvas as a contract, the alternative would be to use the co-created content and transfer it into a Statement of Work supported by a contractual framework including GTCs, Master Service Agreement, SLA, NDA, etc. It is important to know that in order to move quickly, we need to define a basis for discussion that can be improved together with the suppliers, rather than trying to understand and accept their contracts. In RfP2.0 is predominantly contractual from the start, while LAP is predominantly value and outcomes focused.

Image source: Auckland Council

A great example of a new **mindset** is the case of Auckland Council. They saw the benefit of being prepared and started to develop a regulatory framework. Unfortunately, the commercial models offered by the shortlisted vendors were very different and it was impossible to make them fit their proposals into a contractual framework.

Image source: Auckland Council

While the Agile team was discussing how to solve this challenge, the Auckland Council lawyer came up with a strange idea. He said, "We don't have time to read, understand and negotiate 3 different contractual frameworks from vendors.

So what if we just trust?

The members of the Agile delivery team were confused and asked what he meant. The solution was simple, but a masterpiece of thinking outside of the box. They drew up a 3 pager with all the paragraphs that were most important to them and put them at the top of the vendor's contractual framework.

That way they only had to talk to the vendors about 3 pages - a **Minimum Viable Contract** (MvC) if you like.

Execution / Big Room Workshop Pattern

The Execution part of LAP, often initiated through a collaborative event called the Big Room Workshop, and as such, forms the heart of Lean-Agile Procurement. The Big Room Workshop brings the cross-functional team, stakeholder, end-user/-customer from the buyer together with the vendor/partners. It's key to understand that from the vendor/partner side, beside the traditional sales representatives the leadership people with decision competencies must be present. Overall, the specific key potential joint delivery people/team need to attend the Big Room Workshop.

> *Instead of eliminating the less promising offers we ended up improving each proposal and choosing the best one!*
> *— **Eric Chaumette** Managed Delivery Centers Program Management Air France*

To get a sense of what a Big Room Workshop looks like follow the QR code below and watch the recording of a Big Room as a time labs video.

Image source: CKW AG

Having all shortlisted vendors in the same room (in person or virtually) might sound strange and risky. However, it allows to collectively ideate, re-prioritize, adapt, etc. the solutions / proposals / etc. by fostering open dialogue, iterative planning, and visualizing the intermediate results. In addition, it ensures a fair, open and transparent approach to procurement - one of the key tenets of public sector procurement. Lastly, Big Room Workshop structure harness the collective intelligence to drive efficient and responsive execution, ensuring that the procurement journey remains aligned with the principles of agility and value delivery.

The following table gives some insight into the challenge we are trying to solve and the purpose of this pattern:

Table: Lean-Agile Procurement - Execution / Big Room Workshop

Pattern	Description
Challenge	The transactional nature of RfP2.0 and its focus on large paper-based documents that communicate poorly, leaving a lot of room for interpretation and mis-interpretation. In strategic sourcing cases, where the content is often still hypothetical, alignment isn't really possible or takes a lot of time.
PURPOSE of Pattern	The buyer and all potential partners are aligned simultaneously in an open, transparent and fair environment.

Input	- Shortlisted potential partners and Agile delivery team are present with key people especially those that will be involved in delivery - Agenda / Script to achieve the objectives of the Big Room Workshop incl. e.g. Challenges to assess the vendors beyond their product / service - Updated Canvas with all relevant attachments - Draft of an Agile contract framework - Current Roadmap, Product & impediment Backlog with next tasks and risks
Key activity	- Big Room Workshop incl. co-creation of proposal, negotiation, team setup, etc.

Output	- Partner/s awarded a signed contract - Agile Delivery included Collaboration Model agreed and updated - Key stakeholders, end-user/-customer are updated - Roadmap, Product & impediment Backlog with next tasks and risks updated
Key Difference to RfP2.0	The Big Room Workshop is 180 degrees different to a traditional tender as it fosters co-creation, deeper and more complete communications, the use of the collective intelligence across companies. It respects the concerns, IP's of the different vendors and creates a safe environs that allows open and honest collaboration rather than the competitiveness of RfP2.0.

At first, a Big Room Workshop sounds both too good and impossible. For people who feel uncomfortable, we recommend that they lower their expectations/ ambitions and just go for a solution selection, for example.

Image source: Swiss Casinos Group - Big Room Workshop

We usually start the Big Room Workshop by creating alignment:

- what's the project about?
- what are the expected results?
- what's our long-term vision?
- etc.

In the case of Swiss Casinos Group, this alignment was the task of Stefan Meyer, CFO and sponsor of the new ERP system. This often leads to questions from the vendors and in rare cases we have even adopted the business objectives thanks to the input from the crowd.

"This is the fairest contract we've ever agreed on!"
– various parties joined a Big Room Event

One of the most common question we get is how to deal with confidential information, from the vendor/partners as they don't want to share such items as competitive advantage or pricing information, for example. The question of how to develop trust with the vendors is an important one, and needs to be addressed during the preparation. The challenge can be solved quite easily by having these conversations in private break-out rooms. However, it's important to have all vendor/partners in a workshop at the same time, as this gives us the flexibility and opportunity to bring everyone up to date at any time.

Image source: Swiss Casinos Group - Big Room Workshop

The solution, procurement and implementation risk can be significantly reduced in the Big Room Workshop by having both the vendor/partner-side and buyer-side people involved in, and committing to such tasks as the required estimating, creating a solution design, and roadmapping, for example.

Image source: Swiss Casinos Group - Big Room Workshop

The Big Room Workshop is even more powerful, as it enables you to deal with unforeseen circumstances in real time. In one case we realized that we'd forgotten to prepare the software license model, a key cost component in software. As soon as we realized this, we immediately stopped the workshop and asked the 3 vendors/competitors, to co-create the optimal license model for our specific case. To our surprise, they were able to do this in just 15 minutes. At Roche, we even started the Big Room Workshop with a panel, where the senior partners of the 4 invited consultancies talked about the current developments in the market, how they relate to the sourcing case, etc. This set the context as well as the tone.

In one case with the Australian government, it was obvious that no single vendor could provide a solution, so we asked for alliances in the Big Room Workshop. The Big Room Workshop enables and facilitates the ability to adapt, reduce risk, and ensure the right solution for the particular context of the sourcing case.

How to co-create an Agile Contract in less than 1-2 days with multiple parties simultaneously?

We found it to be a good practice to apply to the facilitation of a Big Room Event with Agile practices. As such, we usually Sprint in several iterations through all the topics below. Sprinting allows us to get and share fast feedback and learn for the next iteration. This improves every vendor's results with every iteration and at the end we're able to choose the best overall fit! We have also found, that an Agile Roadmap is as an important appendix to your contract. Then the vendor/partner team can then iterate on it and improve it together with the buyer/customer until it's "Good enough"!

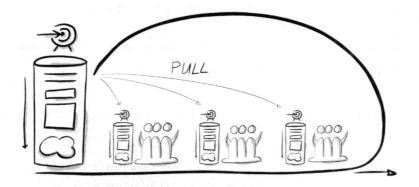

Image source: LAP Alliance Agile Execution of Big Room Workshop

Depending on your preferred Lean-Agile agreement (contract type), you may not need some of the topics below. Also, sometimes a Proof of Concept (PoC) is not appropriate, but I wouldn't miss having the vendor/partners create at least a presentation, or a solution design, or something similar to show the vendor/partner's capability. If we're Sprinting, why not present the results to the real end users from time to time and get their feedback? Alternatively, let the vendors pull their topics via a joint planning and test their commitment right away.

The following table gives an idea of the possible topics that could be included in a Big Room Workshop agenda:

Table: Lean-Agile Procurement - Execution / Big Room Workshop Topics

Topic	Purpose
Introduction	Getting in touch, who's here, in what role
Approach	Agenda incl. Working Agreement for the workshop & Definition of Done (DoD)
Alignment/Context	Vision, business objective of product/service (buyer+vendor/partner(s))
Persona's	Customer segmentation, it's importance & needs
Agile Roadmap	Timeframe for objectives & key deliverables
Proof-of-concept (PoC)	Delivery/Presentation of most challenging aspects
Lean-Agile Agreement	Improving the Agile contract design, its commercial/collaboration model, etc.
Solution	Technical design/-conditions
Estimation	Putting the numbers together & agreeing on risk-share, assumptions, etc.

Demo's	Presentations of intermediate-/results/content for the participants or with the main stakeholders
Peer-feedback	intermediate feedback/decisions

If this is your first big room event, it's recommended to have at least one facilitator who is used to dealing with 20+ people. Also, I always create a script with a detailed estimate for each time slot, so it's more feasible how long it will really take. However, you should always expect and react to the unexpected, as we did in the license model explained earlier where we immediately stopped the workshop and let the 3 competitors design the optimal licensing model together.

The following table gives an idea of other good practices for a Big Room Workshop agenda:

Table: Lean-Agile Procurement - Execution / Big Room Workshop Topics

Practice	Description
Sprinting	Iterating on above topics with joint events such as Sprint Planning, Review, Retro
Fixed Time-boxes	Strict facilitation of time-boxes
PULL	Self-organization of vendor teams
Facilitation	Mix up with various big group facilitation techniques
Co-location	All in 1 room all the time, except for confidential topics private sessions
Transparency	Immediate sharing of new insights
Collaboration	Let the people work together that might become partners and will ship the product/service together
Surprises	To test vendors behavior under stress insert some surprises and pitfalls to understand how vendor/partner(s) react

No Secrets	Put anything on the table you recognize such as bad behavior, strange solution, etc. to clarify it immediately
FUN	Don't forget to make and keep a good atmosphere

Finally, a short management summary for leaders:

- **Investment:** It's worth it spending 1-2+ days with so many people so that they all will be aligned and ready to deliver immediately. Imagine the costs, if they are not!- Incremental sourcing minimizes risk and maximizes business value at the same time!
- **Time-to-Market:** Time-to-Market can only be improved if we change the way we currently work. As a leader you're in the position to enable this and support the business in keeping up with the market demand. On average we estimate a lead time of 2-4 weeks per case (Big Room Event included) and typically see an improvement of 400-800% over traditional approaches!
- **Constraints:** This new way of working doesn't come for free. It requires signifi-

cant support from you as a leader because we need to rethink and bend some of existing processes and policy. However, the idea is not to bypass compliance. The simple fact that we have assembled all subject matter experts e.g. from compliance, procurement, business, etc. in the cross-functional team ensures compliancy through the process. So no worries!

- **Presence:** Your presence as a leader has considerable impact and lends significant importance to the topic and the outcomes. You have the opportunity to show your support by introducing and reinforcing the business objectives, the vision, and by providing your support for the cross-functional team. Your experience during negotiations, critical questions or situations, for example can be instrumental in moving the case forward. Even if you decide to be silent, and let your team run with the initiative, your presence is still very significant to the success of LAP.

I wish you all the best with your application of the Big Room Workshop. Let us know how it went!

Please note: A gentle reminder that a Big Room Workshop is only one of the patterns for solving a particular challenge. There are circumstances in which it isn't needed, or is used in a very minimal way. Think about the initial intended outcome of LAP: If we only had 1 hour, what would we need to know from the vendor/s to select them?

Peer-feedback/-decision

Peer feedback and decision-making constitute a pivotal aspect of Lean-Agile Procurement, embodying the collaborative spirit of agility. In this approach, decisions are made collectively, drawing upon the insights and expertise of the cross-functional team, all key stakeholders and vendors.

> *Decision latency is the enemy of time-to-market*
> *—**Jeff Sutherland**, co-creator of Scrum*

By enabling transparent and iterative peer feedback, organizations not only enhance the quality of procurement decisions but also foster a culture of shared accountability, continuous improvement, and adaptability to changing circumstances, all funda-mental tenets of Lean-Agile Procurement.

The following table gives some insight into the challenge we are trying to solve and the purpose of this pattern:

Table: Lean-Agile Procurement - Peer-Feedback

Pattern	Description
Challenge	The transactional one-pass, bet the farm nature of RfP2.0 leaves parties with a minimum of feedback cycles, often only the final decision, with a lot of back-end risk.
PURPOSE of Pattern	In order to minimize risk and maxi-mize business value for the cus-tomer, the buyer and all potential partners ask for and give constant feedback on the thoughtful sourc-ing and delivery of the product.
Input	- Honest observations, concerns, questions, risks from both buyer and potential partner(s) - Technical & business opinions about the proposed solution, prod-uct or service - Current gut feeling about social & cultural fit

Key activity	Peer feedback in retrospectives throughout the product/partnership lifecycle, e.g. sourcing, big room workshop, delivery.
Output	- Mitigated concerns, risk, questions - Inputs how to adopt collaboration, behavior, or even the product, solution, service
Key Difference to RfP2.0	Compared to an RfP2.0, suppliers only get feedback once, when they are awarded or not. To solve complex problems, we need to ask for/ provide feedback iteratively, not just in sourcing, but throughout the partner lifecycle. This is how we all learn and continuously improve.

In Lean Agile Procurement, we start by defining success or outcome and how we're going to measure it as we move through sourcing and later delivery.

Assessments

Image source: Roche

The high-level assessment criteria used in a strategic sourcing case at Roche show that soft skills, or the social and cultural fit, becomes as important as the hard skills when dealing with complexity.

From output > outcome > impact

In terms of metrics, we should always remember that we're trying to measure the **impact** of the product/service we source. It would be easier to measure output, i.e. whether a, b, c has been delivered. Measuring outcomes are more difficult as it's often lagging. An example would be the satisfaction of the end-user/-customer or the improvement of process efficiency by x% with the new tool, etc. Monitoring and measuring impact is quite new. It focuses on a larger sense such as society, sustainability or the environment. In a conversation with Laurence Pidcock, General Manager NZ Government Procurement, we

138

talked about how procurement can have a bigger positive impact. A low-hanging fruit would be to adopt the selection criteria and, for example, give higher priority to companies with Māori employees. This simple change could encourage companies to employ more Māori, which would solve a lot of other side effects and lead to a better society in New Zealand.

Image Source: SwissCasinos Group - Peer feedback

During the Big Room Workshop, we hold peer feedback sessions as often as necessary, but at least every other hour. The very act of asking/giving feedback to/from each of the vendor/partner fosters a culture of shared accountability, continuous improvement and adaptability to changing circumstances - all fundamental tenets of Lean-Agile Procurement. Our feedback is supported by the metrics. This is a significant departure form RfP2.0 where communications are often limited to the exchange of documents, with little face to face opportunity to provide feedback.

In rare cases, one of the vendor/partners might disqualify themselves. The peer feedback session would be the place to announce this. In one of our cases this actually did happen. So we asked the vendor/partner what he should do - we didn't want to waste his time and ours. To our surprise, the vendor/partner decided to stay, despite knowing he could not win, because they had also learnt so much during the Big Room workshop and were curious to learn more.

The final peer feedback during a Big Room Workshop is also the selection of the partner / product or service. After selection, it's recommended to address any questions or complaints from the non-selected suppliers. If the decision can't be made in the Big Room, it's fair to let them know in the next 1-2 working days.

In highly regulated environments such as government, pharmaceuticals, banking and other sectors, it's often the case that the Agile delivery team does not have the decision-making authority to make the final decision. In these scenarios, our experience has lead us to ensure Agile delivery team co-create the recommendation, instead of options with pros and cons. In one case in the public sector this helped to have a kind of pre-selection including contracts in place, while only waiting for the final committee approvals.

Please note: A gentle reminder that LAP doesn't prescribe what kind of practice to use for peer feedback. However, we have found the 'fist of five' to be very effective.

6. Case Studies

Over the last 7 years, Lean-Agile Procurement has become the global standard in procurement for complex strategic sourcing cases. The LAP Alliance now has a track record in almost every industry and category in both the public and private sectors.

> „In 20 years of Solution Selling Business Software, this was the fastest, most efficient and cost effective partner and solution evaluation. There should definitely be more sourcing cases using Lean-Agile Procurement!"
> – **P. Dragicevic**, Territory Channel Manager BA at Microsoft

In the next chapters we've selected several case studies, two from the private sector and five from the public sector, to demonstrate the power of LAP in more detail and especially in highly regulated environments.

We've also put together some observations, recommendations and opportunities for leaders in government procurement. To this end, we've added an example, to illustrate how LAP can overcome the challenges and risks of a $1 billion public procurement in sourcing new trains.

Sourcing of a Group ERP in 2 Days!

Swiss Casinos Group, Switzerland
www.swisscasinos.ch

Image Source: Swiss Casinos Group

Swiss Casinos is a Swiss gambling and casino company, #1 in the market with 800,000 visits, 580 employees with annual revenues of CHF 160 million. It recently entered the online gambling market and is still on its digital journey.

> *„It's the 4th project concerning an ERP Software I am engaged in, but thanks to Lean-Agile Procurement it's the first time I am convinced before even starting that we will create a good and valuable product for the users."*
> – **Stefan Meyer**, *CFO Swiss Casinos / CEO Swiss Casinos Services AG*

The gaming market is becoming increasingly disrupted, so Swiss Casinos has had to adapt its business model and invest heavily in digitalization. At the end of 2018 the Board of Directors approved the "Shakira" project, that introduced a new ERP software as the next step toward a more digital company. Swiss Casinos had a deadline of January 2020 (less than a year) to complete the delivery and concluded that this date was not feasible using a traditional procurement approach (RfI/RfP). Swiss Casinos decided to try Lean Agile Procurement (LAP) for the first time for their group ERP procurement.

Goals

- Shorten go-to market from 6-12 months to 1-2 months
- Find a new product/partnership/approach to solve current and acute customer needs in an interactive and incremental way
- Test collaborations and products/services with potential partners before signing a contract
- Enable employees to be more self-organized and empowered to make decisions.

Approach & Timing

The core format for implementing Lean-Agile Procurement was based on a two-day workshop where Swiss Casinos co-designed an Agile contract with three suppliers. The workshop actually produced working product increments at the end of each day, which were publicly presented to users from accounting, human resources, procurement, etc.

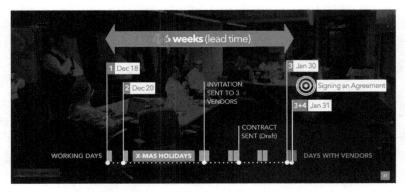

Image Source: Swiss Casinos Group

In addition we set up an empowered, cross-functional product team that had end-to-end competence and responsibility. This meant that the people were working with the new partner team from the outset of the product build. This ensured we had the right expertise in the team, including communications/business/technology/collaboration/purchasing/contracting. Other experts, such as legal, were made available and brought in as needed.

The team worked in 1-week iterations with feedback loops where they presented their results publicly to the client and all stakeholders. We did not use the traditional steering committee approach. In one of the iterations, the team facilitated a 4-hour large group workshop with 20 participants representing all personas/customer segments to capture their real needs and prioritization. Nice-to-have features and capabilities were identified together with the user representatives and were immediately positioned as „out of scope„.

> *"This is the fairest contract we've ever done"*
> – **Lawyer**, *SwissCasinos*

The team leveraged the Lean Procurement Canvas as their main capture tool. This guided them through all the procurement topics and kept them at the right level of detail. For example, the team developed their preferred collaboration/pricing model based on Lean/Agile principles. Together with the team the lawyer and procurement experts drafted an initial Agile contract. One of the statements from that experience was that: "This is the fairest contract we've ever done". This proved to be very useful since all the typical critical legal terms, conditions and considerations such as risk-share, warranty, etc. were addressed early in the process.

Image Source: Swiss Casinos Group

The first two activities, of Initiation and Preparation took three weeks with no involvement of potential partners. Next, we invited the three shortlisted partners for the 4th week for two days. None were given time to prepare in advance. They were expected to show up with the right people to work with our product team, and with the customer. They also needed to bring their sales, legal, and key decision-makers with the authority to work collaboratively with Swiss Casinos to achieve the workshop's intended outcome: A final Agile contract. The buyer team from Swiss Casinos were looking for a team from the vendor/partner that would be consistently engaged, not only in procurement but also the on-going delivery of value over time. Further, the Swiss Casinos were looking for a team with a „cultural-fit". The vendor/

148

partner information package on the meeting was limited to a briefing about the approach, the goal of the 2-day workshop and a copy of the draft Agile contract. Also, the vendor/partners were paid for their participation in this 2-day workshop. This was to ensure the engagement was fair and unbiased. Because Swiss Casinos believed, even though there could only be one winner, that they were getting considerable value from all the vendor/partner participants.

It's important to understand, that LAP uses this vendor/partner/buyer workshop to validate the capabilities and the cultural fit of the vendor/partners.

Image Source: Swiss Casinos Group

The first goal of the 2-day workshop with the three vendor/partners in one room was to jointly co-create an offer from each potential partner. This offer could be agreed to and authorized, and to be ready to immediately start implementing some of the higher priority customer needs.

Thanks to the Lean Procurement Canvas we had a summary of the collaboratively developed Agile contract. This was critical, as it provided everyone a clear understanding of the vision / the customer needs / timing / collaboration / pricing model, bounding conditions, etc. Questions and risks were resolved within minutes. For example, it turned out that the License Model is crucial, yet the specific detail was yet to be developed. To deal with this, we asked the 3 vendor/partners to co-develop the optimal License Model for this case which they accomplished collaboratively in just 15 minutes! Next, they were immediately tasked to negotiate the best license costs with their respective Microsoft Partner Manager. This task took only an additional 15 minutes to complete as well!

Image Source: Swiss Casinos Group

The second objective of the workshop was to run a proof of concept in parallel to further assess the capability and the collaboration of the vendor/partner teams. At the end of each day the vendor/partners presented in a public review, what they had developed that day, and it was shared with all the stakeholders. Questions were answered, and feedback was given to each vendor/partner. At the beginning of each day, each vendor/partner committed to what they expected to achieve by the end of the next day. This allowed the client to gain insight into how each potential partner planned and discussed their work, and to review what was achieved.

Beside creating the offer, the vendor/partner development teams built proof-of-concepts designed to fulfill the most important customer needs, and

151

current challenges in the legacy ERP system. The results were also presented in the public reviews.

As we constantly gave feedback to all the vendor/partners it was easy to assess at any time the capabilities and feasibility of the vendor/partner solutions and their cultural fit. This led to fierce competition in all aspects of the procurement process. For example, the vendor/partners proposed their own innovative „outside the box" ideas, in addition to the requested needs in order to make their respective offers more attractive.

Image Source: Swiss Casinos Group

The most important success criteria for LAP is to involve the people doing the work with the outcome/vision. Namely, WHY we need this product, the personas and their needs/WHAT their solution/services, and HOW it would be beneficial or provide value. We let vendor/partners estimate the user stories (Agile technique to describe the need from the customer's perspective) including level of effort and schedule estimates in consideration of the complexity of their product and their approach. This co-creative approach was also the basis for their respective cost ceiling estimations, and schedules, as well as the high level business objectives that were addressed in the Agile contracts. This process offered the buying team to better evaluate vendor/partner performance and to better understand the socio-cultural values of the respective vendor/partners in real time.

The winning vendor/partner decision was taken by the product team at the end of the 2nd day. We communicated the decision directly to all vendor/partners, and dealt with all their questions and/or concerns. Then we signed a contract with the winning vendor/partner.

Swiss Casinos was looking for a long term partnership, however the contracts were iterative. The first one was for just the initial 6 months period and could be terminated at any time, by either party without penalty. This was to ensure continued engagement and investment by both parties in the partnership. The re-evaluation approach was simple, go/no-go renewal, at the end of the 6-month process or as needed. In addition, the winning vendor/partner team invited a person from another vendor/partner team to join their team as he was a great performer and a nice person too!

There were no further delays, the pilot solution was sketched out, the Agile contract had been finalized, therefore, the winning vendor/partner team could just start working immediately, on the 3rd day, without further ramp-up or delays.

Metrics

The following key success metrics were used in the sourcing case with the Swiss Casinos Group:

- **Time to Market** - 4x Faster (4 Weeks instead of 6 Months)
- **Savings** - 80% Less Costs (Focus on the most important modules first)
- **Decision to Contract** - 10x Faster (Same Day instead of 1-2 Months)
- **Efforts** - 50% Less (2.1 FTE instead of 4-5 FTE)

- **Happiness** - 9 of 10 Recommendation Rate From both, the Buyer & Supplier

The results were astonishing, as we achieved a new procurement World Record, that was recognized by Procurement Leaders with the World Procurement Award 2020!

Business Outcome

Beside the metrics the Swiss Casinos Group reported the following business outcomes applying Lean-Agile Procurement:

- Increased business value by involving users throughout, e.g. during the large group workshop and public reviews.
- Staffing and empowering the x-functional team, resulting in a significant reduction in the lead time to complete the work. The team had end-to-end product lifecycle skills that enabled them to make the sourcing decision.
- The workshop also provided an opportunity to significantly reduce social and tech-

nical risks by providing an opportunity to validate the product, the service.

- The collaboration and validation of vendor/partner competencies and people.
- Based on customer-driven needs, the team worked together to design appropriate solutions that would fit within the business objectives and cost framework. This significantly reduced the financial risk, cost and staff time required to complete the task.
- Time-to-market was significantly accelerated as the new Agile team - consisting of buyer & seller - was able to start work on the 3rd day.
- Contractual risks were significantly reduced as all critical co-created aspects of the Agile contract were made transparent and updated immediately. In addition, the Agile contract ensured the necessary flexibility in all details.

How Agile is changing an Industry & Lives!

APA Group, Australia

Image source: APA Group

APA is a leading Australian energy infrastructure business. Henriette introduced us to how applying Agile is currently changing a whole Industry and also her Life!-In other words she's talking us through how Lean Agile Procurement has helped to shape significant change in individuals, teams, organizations and supply chains within the energy industry.

The following is a transcript of the interview with Henriette Kampfer, Category Specialist APA Group interviewed by Marcus Ward Certified LAP Trainer and Agile Coach:

Can you tell us a little bit about Yourself?

I'm in Adelaide, Australia and I've been in procurement for more than 20 years. In the past three years I've been in a procurement role in the APA Group. But it's really over the past 12 months that I've experienced a shift happening. Inside me basically on how best to do procurement. And that's why we are here today, Marcus.

And APA Group, tell us a little bit about your company.

So currently we have across APA and our asset owner, close to 2.2 million gas customers. And we perform more than 12 million meter reads annually, however, We are using old 20th century equipment and we are manually reading our meters.

The energy market in Australia has shifted with the introduction of electricity smart meters, and this reshaped our thinking about what our customers really need. We have a very ambitious vision: Our vision is a digital meter future where our customers can monitor and control their gas consumption and where they will see the gas industry as an integral part of the energy decisions. And all of this we wanna achieve by 2030.

So what I'm hearing there, big company, lots of complexity in terms of size and shape but bold, ambitious vision as well. Just like to ask you how Agile is APA to deal with this level of change in digital transformation?

Well, if there was a scale from one to 10, We would be less than one. We had no experience with Agile at APA at all. Our traditional approach has just been, that we spend enormous amounts of effort and resources creating these detailed specifications and then, base it on our past experience. We do not look at the future and we do not consult with suppliers at all.

And little thought is really given, as to what it should it be like? And that's just the way it's always been.

So, you've got this big vision, what you want to aim for, but, so this journey about changing industries, like how have you got to this point?

So, the expiry of our existing contracts are looming and we are faced with this complex challenge with the market changing and reshaping. And we just realized that our traditional approach for procurement has been fit for purpose, it's fine for other parts of our organization, but in terms of this complex problem that we had, we really needed to make a shift and needed to make a change in how we are doing it.

And APA afforded us that opportunity to do something different, to try something different so that we can get a different result and we can move away from the same old, same old.

And what have your learnings been along the way?

So look, with our limited approach we appointed our Lean Agile coaches, which is where you came in, Marcus, and you've been guiding us all along our process. And we started by establishing our cross-functional delivery team and our main focus has been on culture first and with that, we started with a team agreement, we also reduced all the heavy documentation that we used to have in the past, to a project on a page, and we focused on what was needed today, tomorrow and 2030. So we made that shift towards the future. We then posed our problem to the supply market to determine what is the optimal model for us to move away from our old equipment. And Marcus, we actually asked our suppliers to tell us why they should be invited to attend our Big Room Workshop, and we focused on the cultural fit with the vendor/partners.

And only best fit suppliers were shortlisted and invited to date. We've done one Big Room event where it really turned out very good practice to apply Agile practices to it too. We had sprints that we did and we had several iterations on the product specification, on the roadmaps and on the pricing estimates.

This allowed us for fast feedback and we actually managed to get our first estimates after only four hours of supplier engagements. Now we can work together with our suppliers and we can do some more iterations and improve it together until it's good enough. And then, we can in the end, choose the best of it.

Incredible story. So moving from months to hours for estimates?

That's right. Well, my journey started about a year ago in the beginning of 2020, joining the LAP training. And I think my biggest learning has been the realization that my role as a procurement person has to change.

I need to become a procurement enabler. It means that I have to create an opportunity between the suppliers and my internal stakeholders to work together to solve this complex problem. And the real shift started within me, when I realized that my role is more that of an orchestra conductor bringing all the elements together, the suppliers and the stakeholders in for it to form a wonderful melody out of the process. I do recall that it was really hard for us as a biased team to shift and to define our why, our true north, and to set out clearly our goals and key result areas.

We also identified personas and prioritized our needs, and we eagerly pasted all of our thoughts on stickies, on our Lean Procurement Canvas. And all of this definitely was a first, not only for me, but for my stakeholders and the bias team, but we persisted. We helped each other along the way, and as we got into this regular rhythm, Our focus really started to move away from specifications towards what the end customer really wants.

And as a team, we are now pioneering the future and our team has actually become the main asset for our organization as opposed to just the process. And it's really nice to hear if our project manager says, He doesn't wanna go back to his day job or the feed-back that we received from our meeting supervisor has been that he truly enjoyed the process.

People seldom enjoy a procurement process and as procurement in APA, we are really blazing a trail for the first time ever with our Big Room work-shops, having suppliers in the same room with us and co-creating proposals is really new. When I first mentioned this to my peers and to legals, they thought it's impossible to have, not only to have sup-pliers in one room, but to move fast through a process of completing a contract that normally would take months.

It's really truly a unique opportunity to have the suppliers and the buyer, the bioTE in one room, and you just remove that whole bottleneck of information sharing out of the way. But fundamentally what has changed for us is really the shift in the culture. It's now one of trust and cooperation.

It's based on partnership and shared values. Yes, we are still focusing on the hard facts like quality and costs, but the behavior of the suppliers in a real life situation has been really important to us, and it's shown us cultural fit and the consequence of is really very visible. It's impacted on APA's market reputation and the loyalty of our partners because they are really seeing us as a key customer.

But it's also clearly visible on the motivation and the performance of each team member if of our team. So for me, I actually have a vision of the future where the procurement team and the function can really become a strategic enabler to APA. To keep us relevant and for us to stay in business.

And it's really a truly a rare opportunity that we have now to influence the gas industry in Australia with our partners.

You mentioned your learnings as a Coach?

Oh you know, it's been an incredible journey for me and I've gotta say, my greatest reward is being here today with you and seeing your journey from when we first started the initiative and those early workshops.

I run regular retrospectives on myself and you know, three big learnings that I picked up first one was meeting people where they're at.

I had the luxury of working with some very progressive organizations with forward ways of thinking. And for me it was a great adventure to work with APA and go back to basics and encourage this alignment between all parties. Achieving that is why clear upfront discussion have really helped the team to accelerate as we got into the latest stages and also avoid some of those difficult conversations around conflicting opinions.

Secondly, feedback, again, environments I've worked in feedback was just second nature to us. Whereas within this industry this concept of transparent feedback is one that's growing and evolving. So helping people to adopt that and seeing the benefits that come from it. And thirdly communicate, communicate, communicate.

So even though we had a really good structured plan around communication and we felt like we have captured every stakeholder, you can always do more. And we learned that almost at the 11th hour before going into our big room workshop. So never underestimate the power of bringing people on board and getting them comfortable in the process.

Maybe share some of the Feedback from Suppliers as well?

Yes, we had some good feedback. I think the biggest difference for our partners has been the change in the set of values. We are now applying Agile values that are transparency, honesty, and commitment.

The concept of sharing in the Big Room Workshop has been accepted differently across the supply base. Some suppliers were further along the Agile journey than others, and some had some catching up to do, but the willingness has been there to share and we've seen that already with our first big room and with all the suppliers participating in that one Session with each other. Some of the feedback, real-time feedback that we've received from the suppliers were things like, it's our first at all experience in procurement. We've never done this before and the feedback across our team is that it's a resounding positive experience. So through this process, we've really, I believe, increased APA's reputation as a customer of choice.

Suppliers wanna work with us, they like the process and they like being in this. With us in this project and in this journey.

Awesome. Where should people start?

Well, as a participant, you may be thinking, where do I start? And all I can say is that I've been in the same boat as you a year ago. I can still recall Mirko's voice, clearly saying in the training: „What are the small things that you can start doing tomorrow that will make a change!" All those little steps add up to this big difference.

Or perhaps you may wanna follow our journey and get some help along the way. And adopt a coach that can help you. But whatever you decide to do, it's really well worth it. This is a change and the results and the impacts on your company will be greatly different to what you've experienced before.

Thank you.

The interview was recorded and presented the first time at a CIPS.org Meetup in Switzerland:

Image Source: APA Group - Interview with Henriette Kampfer

Business Outcome

- Agile is more than just a new way of working, it changes lives of the people involved
- Instead of just following the sourcing process procurement became part of innovation, with e.g. impact on how people in Australia see their energy consumption
- the inclusive approach and applying Scrum to the core-team consisting of all capabilities / functions needed helped to align with the strategy faster and to find the optimal partner

Awarded success Story with the Dunedin City Council

Dunedin City Council, New Zealand
www.dunedin.govt.nz

Image source: Dunedin Council and Portt with WCC awards. Image Source: Dunedin City Council.

The Dunedin City Council won an award for Outstanding Cooperation & Collaboration at the 2023

World Commerce and Contracting (Asia Pacific) Innovation and Excellence Awards – Congratulations!

> „I've awarded many, many contracts, but I've never been hugged by a vendor at the end of it, when I told him that he won the contract. That tells you something."
> – **Serge Kolman**, Procurement & Contracts Manager, Dunedin City Council

The award was for a Lean-Agile Procurement (LAP) process the Dunedin City Council (DCC) undertook to source a Contract Lifecycle Management System, and the outstanding way DCC and the successful vendor/partner, Portt, collaborated through the lean-agile process to achieve their goals.

Procurement at Dunedin City Council

The Dunedin City Council represents the people that live in Ōtepoti Dunedin, New Zealand. The DCC's purpose is to enable decision making by and on behalf of communities, and to promote social, economic, environmental and cultural wellbeing.

Public dollar spend makes up a significant proportion of the NZ economy, including spend from local government organizations like DCC. The DCC has an important responsibility to ensure it spends rate payers funds prudently through its procurement processes – in an open, transparent and accountable way. DCC follows the NZ Government Rules of Procurement. When procuring Goods or Services, they use the NZ Government Electronic Tendering Site (GETS) to list all open market tenders. This site enables registered users to electronically review and respond to all current open market tenders being conducted by the Council.

One of DCC's procurement rules is that procurement with a cumulative value of over $100,000 requires an open and competitive process, which typically takes over three months.

Why Dunedin City Council used a Lean-Agile approach

Previously, DCC had faced challenges sourcing Software as a Service (SaaS) through a traditional open market Request for Proposal (RFP) approach, with a few complex SaaS contracts resulting in vendor/partners that could not deliver on requirements.

The DCC was going through a Contract Management improvement project, which included sourcing a Contract Lifecycle Management (CLM) system and wanted to ensure the same situation did not occur again as with previous SaaS procurements. This was a strategically important project for DCC, and therefore success was paramount.

It was important that the CLM system sourced met the Council's requirements to ensure the success of the wider Contract Management improvement project.

When DCC was looking for a way to maximize the success of the procurement process to ensure the right outcomes were achieved, they began looking into the Lean-Agile Procurement approach as an option.

Dunedin City Council's Lean-Agile Approach

To source the CLM system, DCC decided the contract was complex enough to use a Lean-Agile Procurement approach.

DCC undertook a two stage procurement process.

Stage one was an open market Registration of Interest, using GETS[1]. This was done for two reasons:

1. To comply with DCC's Procurement and Contract Management Policy.
2. We didn't know what we didn't know and didn't want to miss out on new or emerging technology that we hadn't uncovered through our market research (aka we had FOMO!).

Following stage one, DCC shortlisted three vendor/partners for the second stage of the CLM Software procurement.

Stage two was a two day workshop 'Big Room Event' utilizing Lean-Agile Procurement techniques. As it was DCC's first Lean-Agile Procurement process, we engaged Ross Darrah from Pareto Toolbox, as an expert in LAP, to assist and coach the DCC team through the process.

---

[1] Government Electronic Tendering Service (GETS) https://www.gets.govt.nz/ExternalIndex.htm

Image source: Dunedin City Council - DCC and Pareto Toolbox presenting to Lean Agile Procurement Canvas during the DCC LAP Process.

It was acknowledged that LAP was a new process for vendor/partners and DCC stakeholders, and particularly as this was being conducted in a public sector environment, probity was absolutely crucial. The DCC team and vendor/partners were therefore coached and fully briefed on LAP, to ensure full understanding of the process and to give confidence to all stakeholders and vendor/partners that they were involved in a 'safe' process which was fair, transparent and complied with required public sector regulations and probity standards.

The DCC team fully embraced the LAP process and focused during the two days on getting to know the shortlisted vendor/partners. It was important for DCC to understand how the respective vendor's approach would work for DCC and the capabilities of their CLM solutions.

During the two days of the LAP process, DCC and shortlisted vendor/partners approached the event as an opportunity to start building the relationships.

Business Outcomes Achieved using the Lean-Agile Approach

In adopting a Lean-Agile Procurement approach, DCC achieved accelerated decision making and cut down the time and cost required for vendor/partners to do business with DCC. It also enabled strong relationship building between DCC and the successful vendor/partner – setting a solid foundation for the delivery of the work.

Image source: Dunedin City Council - Serge Kolman, DCC Procurement and Contracts Manager presenting to vendor/partners on day one.

The CLM solution was delivered on time and within budget. The success of this contract can be attributed to the innovative procurement approach, effective project delivery, and the willingness of DCC staff to try new ways of working that benefit DCC, its vendor/partners, and the Dunedin communities they work for.

There were some doubts voiced by vendor/partners prior to the event, as this was the first Lean-Agile process DCC and the vendor/partners had participated in. However, the feedback from staff and all vendor/partners involved was overwhelmingly positive - even from the vendor/partners who were not successful!

Key Learnings, Tips and Takeaways

Investment Logic Mapping

Once the CLM software contract was awarded, and as part of the implementation phase, DCC undertook an investment logic mapping (ILM) process with the successful vendor/partner, Portt.

The ultimate aim of the ILM process was to get to the core of the problems we are trying to solve by developing problem statements and identifying the benefits of solving those problems.

Image Source: Dunedin City Council. - Natalie Strong, DCC Procurement Advisor and LAP facilitator updating the LAP canvas during canvas review with DCC staff and shortlisted vendor/partners.

DCC found this process valuable, and they would in future undertake an ILM exercise with key staff and stakeholders before they went through a Lean-Agile Procurement process, as this would inform the canvas (true north) and User Stories by developing problem statements and can be used to measure success of Lean-Agile process.

Working with Vendor/Partners to solve Problems

DCC found it very valuable to have the ability to talk through issues and challenges with vendor/partners, who then demonstrated how they could help solve these problems in real time.

Two Days vs Three Days

DCC felt like they would benefit from one more day, to feel less rushed.

A great outcome can be achieved by doing a Lean-Agile process in two days, but DCC felt like they would get a bit more out of the process if an extra day was included.

Online vs In-Person

Lean-Agile Procurement works best with people in the room, online presence is fine but to be really successful DCC found that physical presence was best.

Tips for other Procurement Leaders

Embrace the process. DCC have found Lean-Agile Procurement to be a really useful tool to have in the procurement toolbelt for the right project.

Ensuring you engage early with decision makers within your environment is essential to the success of the process. Engage early to enlist the support you need (including from decision makers with financial authority) and to enable and achieve the full benefits and potential of a Lean-Agile process.

Time Management & Peer Feedback

A key learning from the Lean-Agile Procurement event was the importance of time management. As already stated, there was a lot to achieve in two days, meaning that sticking to agreed timeframes was of utmost importance. To mitigate this challenge, we ensured that vendor/partners were clear about time-frames up front and this was reinforced throughout the event. In addition, vendor/partners (and DCC stakeholders) were kept on time by using a timer and alarm. This 'refereeing' of the event ensured that the time was maximized.

The strict keeping of time added an additional benefit. It ensured there was sufficient time to provide immediate feedback to vendor/partners to ensure they knew where they stood and made the event a success. This also ensured respect was given to vendor/partners, that is they were held to time but they were provided with feedback on where they needed to improve.

FLASH - Learnings from a $1.5 BN Challenged-based Procurement in the US Government

Department of Homeland Security, USA - Shared by Josh Seckel, former Chief Applied Technology, USCIS

Image Source: google streetview

Prior to 2016, The Department of Homeland Security (DHS) had been using a contract called Eagle 2 for many years to procure software delivery services. In general, the speed of the process to acquire was not effective or efficient as it often resulted in significant delays to the start of work as well as locked in system requirements before teams even began to look at the problem. There are many awardees on Eagle who all can compete for each task that is awarded with DHS. In 2016, there was a decision to try something new. US Citizenship and Immigration Services had already been experimenting with innovative ways of procuring involving orals and technical demonstrations and challenges. This new procurement for DHS would extend that to a Blanket Purchase Agreement for all of DHS in a vehicle called FLASH (Flexible Agile Services for the Homeland) for a total of $1.5B dollars. A total of 8-12 awardees would be chosen to ensure high quality companies and to shorten task order award times.

> *"Please continue doing such collaborative approaches in procurement"*
> — **Vendors** *involved in the challenged-based procurement*

There were two steps to this procurement. The first step was a voluntary video which was evaluated on relatively simple criteria and a response from the government was provided if it was recommended that you continue as a Prime. Many companies submitted videos through the process and all received a response. The instructions were explicit that the video was not to be overproduced and that using a phone for recording was sufficient. This was to keep costs down among potential vendors. Following the video, a technical challenge was held. For the technical challenge, DHS invited all participating teams to bring a team to create a basic application in collaboration with the government provided Product Owner. Each team was given the same product backlog and all Product Owners were provided with training to reduce any deviation from the government. Each team came into the DHS offices for the 4 hour coding challenge. Most had already created the infrastructure and general containers that they would use throughout the challenge. A few even brought servers as backup in case there was an issue with internet connection. The final code repositories were accessible to the government for all teams and DHS performed code review in near real time. Each day, there were 6-8 companies that performed the challenge, with over 100 total companies ultimately going through the process. During the code challenge, the evaluators observed each team working through rotating rooms, getting feedback from the PO, and having certain defined debriefs.

Image source: YouTube

At the end of the 5 weeks of challenges, the additional work to review the past performance and pricing were performed. In total, it was 3 months from the first challenge to announcing the 13 winners. This was one higher than intended, but were the best of the companies and all could have done outstanding work. Because of the federal procurement cycles, there were several protests that were filed following the announcement. In general, the federal procurement process has been designed to limit the probability of successful protests. Because of the new processes that were being followed to move to more technical evaluation, eventually, the decision was made to cancel FLASH as the protest was likely to result in a loss for the government. The decision to cancel was best described as waterfall documentation in an agile procurement process as several of the documents were changed after being submitted which would have resulted in the loss. The decision was also made to cancel rather than to allow the FLASH vehicle to have less than the small number of the best companies. Watering down FLASH to award to more companies to avoid the protest would not have met the mission needs of DHS.

Despite ultimately canceling FLASH, there are a lot of lessons that were learned from the process. First, the use of technical challenges and not just relying on a written proposal improved results. This change is now used more across the federal government and increases the probability of getting high quality companies. Second, performing experiments is important in procurement and then expanding them. FLASH may have been too large of a jump from the USCIS experiments, and the need to continue experimenting is vital to finding the right companies. DHS continues to have a Procurement Innovation Lab that delivers and encourages experimentation across DHS and into the rest of government. Third, having the technical competence on the evaluation team is vital and requires that skillset within the acquiring workforce, even if not at the same scale as the contracted work. The use of USDS for

FLASH was necessary for DHS to complete this procurement in this way and continuing to build those skills across the government is important to the continued success.

For further reading and interesting viewpoints of the FLASH procurement check out: https://tinyurl.com/dhs-FLASH

How the Hospital in Stockholm was newly built on Time, on Budget and has also saved Värmland County Council $300 Million

Värmland County Council, Sweden

Image source: whitearkitekter.com

Karlstad Hospital has procured new construction and extension in order to conduct effective care with a budget of about $105 million. The new construction was built on time, on budget and was ready for business on Day 1. The hospital has also saved Värmland County Council $300 million. The secret?-Agile contracts, partnering and fully focusing on the target. So what created the conditions for success? We interviewed Lars Nilsson, the Head of Procurement at Karlstad Hospital.

Big thanks to agilakontrakt.se for sharing and translating this awesome case from Swedish into English!

Interview with Lars Nilsson, Property Manager @ Värmland County Council held and translated by members of the conference board, published on ag-ilakontrakt.se:

Tell us a little about Karlstad Hospital

The Central Hospital in Karlstad suffered from severe indoor environment problems and huge overcrowding since the early 90's. To address these problems, we needed both renovation and new construction. For reasons of capacity, healthcare operations could not simply be evacuated from the existing buildings. We needed to find new ways to ensure that health care operations could be continued safely in parallel with the construction.

The first rebuilding/refurbishment phase comprised about 25,000 sq. meters. We have used the same approach for the construction of facilities for medical services and internal medical care of about 24 000 sq. meters, new psychiatry premises of approximately 13,000 sq. meters, a new surgery building of 26,000 sq. meters and we continued rebuilding and refurbishing about 30,000 sq. meters of care premises in Karlstad.

The construction projects entailed huge economic investments, that is why it required a careful quality assessment of the economic circumstances in order to make all involved parties feel reassured.

What made you choose the "Partnering" Model for Procurement?

It seemed absurd to us that the problems we were facing could be unique to us. Surely we were not alone. We have seen precedents in England where hospitals have started to work in a new and different way in new construction projects. The **clients agreed with the contractors upfront about the profit** they would need to make to take on a building project. The care business, the contractors and planners then work closely together to seize all opportunities **to create maximum patient benefit** within the financial constraints. With our Swedish law as a starting point, we tried to create conditions for something similar in Karlstad. Sure, some think it was a gamble, but we were convinced that we had no alternative and we did not really know what "partnering" was all about.

You did not choose the traditional fixed-Price Contract, Why not?

For the rebuilding project, it was not possible to provide the clear conditions needed for a fixed-price contract. Given the poor condition of the buildings, we were not sure of the best order in which the projects should be implemented. Once we were able to determine which sub-projects were the most acute, we wanted to take advantage of all opportunities to create the best conditions for health care operations. So we allowed those who were to physically do the work of designing this as closely as possible, to have a dialogue with the people who would operate in the premises. We wanted every project participant's focus to be 100% directed towards creating the most optimal care in our new hospital, rather than seeking to maximize one's own economic gains. All of this would take place in an environment where everyone felt safe. We met both our financial objectives and our delivery dates.

Lookin back, what was the Outcome?

OPERATIONALLY

If we look at the operational outcome, there are three points I want to emphasize:

We succeeded in creating two new and innovative solutions that made the premises well suited to the care that would be conducted and to have a **low maintenance cost**. For example, by using smart materials, we have minimized the maintenance disruptions to the care business.

We have also **found good solutions to energy issues** that have reduced our need to purchase energy. As a reference, in 1999, Värmland County Council purchased the most energy of all county councils in Sweden per square meter of floor space. In 2011, Värmland County Council bought the least. This **saved Värmland County Council some $250 to $300 million** over a 10-year period when compared with other similar local stocks for care (similar hospitals). We have a registered patent in heating as a result of the project. This change is not merely the result of having made good decisions in construction projects. Rather, it is the culmination of the efforts of many people in focusing on efficient energy use. Värmland County Council now has low local costs compared to other premises in which care is conducted to a similar standard.

TIME AND BUDGET

We have **kept all our schedules** and we have also **saved quite a few million Euros** compared to initial budgets. The Operation building was completed **four months before** actual scheduled use (built between 2011 and 2016). The execution phase only took **40-70% of the normal time** for comparable projects.

QUALITY

We chose our materials wisely to minimize the use of chemicals in sensitive areas such as the Neonatal Department (for premature babies). **The Operation building** which has just been put into use was *awarded the "Lead Healthcare Gold" building classification.**

We would not have been able to achieve this had we taken other approaches such as using contractor forms. The difference was due to the fact that we always chose materials that have characteristics best suited to the situation, rather than purely based on economic incentives for the vendor.

DESIGN AND CONSTRUCTION

We have also innovated in the development of new construction techniques over time. A small but concrete example is how we solved the logistics of fastening pipes and conduits for water, gas, electricity and heat when the new rooms were being built. Since pipes are usually mounted a bracket at a time, it can be harder and harder for the contractor down the line to access the wall or ceiling to attach the next pipe or conduit. In our case, we innovated a new way of work which allowed the first contractor to create mounts that would work for all types of pipes and conduits, which makes it both faster and smoother for subsequent construction workers to do their jobs.

An important factor for this was that we were able to make decisions on the spot, as soon as we discovered that conditions had changed. If we find on inspection that the existing walls were in worse condition then we believed, the staff in place could make decisions on the spot about the changes that the project needed to make. **No need to wait for**

decisions to be made in steering groups, we could move to action on the spot.

The time between completing half of the quality assured space is usually extremely short, like 1-2 days. In a typical project, the time between the completed building and inspection can take anywhere from 6 to 12 months.

As you can see, we innovated in several areas, from the way health care business is conducted to energy and building technology.

What are the Key Factors behind the Success?

I want to highlight three factors:

1ST

The first important factor is that we have been able to choose appropriate skills, partners and materials most suited to solve the business problems at hand, without anyone having a personal interest in the choices made. It has been made possible because vendors know what they will earn on the project upfront and that both parties have found it reasonable. As for financial compensation, all participants in the project can put 100% of their energy on solving business problems instead of pushing for their own more expensive solutions in order to maximize gain.

2ND

The second factor is our power control. We set up clear business goals we want to achieve early on and we continuously monitor how we were reaching our goals during the project. This allows us to adapt the solution to business problems instead of the other way around. It may sound obvious, but in reality, it's very difficult to achieve. For the goals to be effective, they had to be formulated to be easily comprehensible, actively followed up and acted upon.

3RD

The third factor is the use of prototyping and the fact that the buildings were built step by step. We did not build all of the buildings all at once, but one at a time. It enabled us to benefit from what we've learned from building one building to the next.

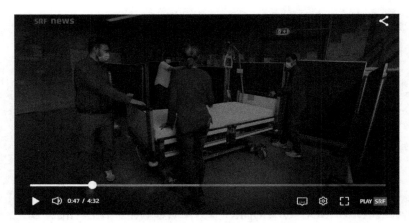

Image source: Srf.ch - Prototyping for the new Lucerne Hospital

We used prototyping for many types of rooms, from the operating room to the restrooms.

- **Step 1:** we model the building throughout and the rooms in 3D.
- **Step 2:** we create prototypes of the rooms in full scale, equipped with the intended equipment. This allows doctors and nurses to try out real life scenarios and make adjustments to the room in order to find the optimal setup for smooth operation.
- **In the final step**, the real room is built.

But don't you know how to build a Toilet?

To build a toilet is quite simple. But how do you adapt that to the space outside or to a number of different care situations? Usually, such a room is designed by an architect with limited experience of care situations. This means that they may not always be optimal when used in real life.

Let's talk a little about Procurement. What did you procure in Terms of Performance, Skills & Abilities?

In practice, we procured resources and knowledge in several areas. In parallel, we made sure to build up the client's skills so that they could have meaningful dialogues with contractors and manage the project.

Can you describe the Criteria for selecting Vendors? How much Weight was attributed to Economics and how much to other Factors?

The financial part is about 20%. The other 80% is made up of knowledge, quality and competence.

What did the Economic Model look like?

It's a twofold economic model. The first was to eliminate all economic and short-term incentives. We simply removed the issue of economics from the table. The second was to ensure that the vendors (construction companies) remained within the framework laid out.

Compensation is broken down into fixed and variable. For the moving part, we pay the net cost for all expended time and materials, without markup. Examples would be all of the participant's salary or purchase cost of materials net of contractor discounts. To ensure transparency, it is a requirement that all parties work with open books.

The fixed part is a supplement to the moving part. It covers central administrative overhead costs and the profit margins of contractors. Contractors would bid on the profit margin percentage. To avoid frivolous bids, we specified a percentage range based on the industry average. The result is that the contractor knows what they will earn on the project upfront and that it is reasonable.

How did you estimate the financial Framework for the Project?

The project is divided into phases. The contract covers the vendor/partner for both Phase 1 and Phase 2. Legally however, the order letter (range) has to be on hand for Phase 2 to be launched.

Phase 1 - Effect	Order Letter	Phase 2 - Implementation

Here the business objectives and the solution is designed in 3D. It gives us a rough estimate of the time and the material scope. We validate the solutions we come up with to see if the client's goals are met or not. For us to move on to the next phase, we need to be confident that we can meet the business requirements as well within our time and financial constraints. Options and Obligations Phase 1 provides an opportunity for the client to implement Phase 2, but not an obligation. To move to the next phase, an Order Letter is created.

The Order Letter indicates the final range for Phase 2. Here we get a more detailed picture of the total cost and project planning. The purchaser has the option to terminate the project if the deviation proves to be too great. The vendor does not however have the option to pull out.

Purchaser's goals are broken down into project goals, and then further into targets for each construction partner participant in the project. The solution is implemented during this phase. The economy is monitored continuously. The project objectives are monitored as part of the project plan 2 times per year. There is also a built-in risk sharing model for all participants. If the variable costs have a variance of more than 5% (which in turn impacts central administration costs and profit), this variance is then deducted from the profit mar-

Are there other Clauses of Importance in the Tender Documentation?

Here are some clauses worth mentioning:

- The first is that the contractors agree to use **open books** to ensure financial transparency and that all forms of discounts that are somehow linked to the project business is returned to the project.
- The other is that the turnkey **contractor must procure their vendors with the same contract terms**. The whole supply chain, from the general contractor to smaller building shops (architects, craftsmen, planners), must follow the same rules.
- The third is a bit more quirky. We have a **loyalty declaration** the CEO of the contractor must sign. In short, it says that the CEO agrees that his employees are expected to **make choices that benefit the project, even if these conflict with the wishes of the employer**. It may sound drastic, but the project puts great trust in the participants' ability to make decisions

and it is important that they feel secure that they can be loyal to the goals of the project. The vendor/partner's willingness to sign the declaration of loyalty is a criterion in the tender documentation.

The loyalty declaration clause was necessary to solve a practical problem. We observed that knowledgeable people whom we trust to find the right solutions hesitated to make the right choices for the project for fear of being at odds with their employers.

The Financial Incentives for Delivering on Time is not very strong. What then is the Incentive for Participants to overcome Difficulties and to Innovate during the Project?

We must not forget a very strong incentive for every participant in the project - to make a difference. We put a lot of work into making sure that everyone in our project understood the effect of the goals we set and how they contribute to making this happen. This allowed every participant to feel proud that they made a difference.

How Swiss Federal Railways reduced Complexity in Critical Procurement Projects

Swiss Federal Railways, Switzerland
www.sbb.ch

Image Source: Swiss Federal Railways

The citizens of Switzerland and the people at Swiss Federal Railways are proud of the quality of their service. Switzerland has one of the best-developed public transport networks in the world. Almost any part of the country can be reached by bus or by train - even remote mountain areas[2]. The Swiss travel more by train than any other nation in the world, clocking up an average of 2,400 km per person every year within Switzerland[3]. Trains are always

---

2   https://www.swissinfo.ch/eng/public-transport-in-switzerland/29081612

3   https://www.eda.admin.ch/aboutswitzerland/en/home/wirtschaft/verkehr/verkehr---fakten-und-zahlen.html

state-of-the-art and on time, with services running every 15 to 30 minutes. 34,200 employees form the backbone of the Swiss economy, transporting more than 1.16 million passengers and 180,000 tonnes of goods every day.

> *Lean-Agile Procurement is the future of contemporary strategic purchasing. Simple, fast and successful!*
> *–* ***Jan-Patrick Willmes****, Head of Center of E-Excellence Supply Chain Management SBB CFF FFS*

In this chapter we'd like to share two stories with the Swiss Federal Railways.

1. Pilot to overcome the Challenges of „over"-Specification in the Procurement of new Trains
2. Pilot for the Procurement of a customized Software for the Visualization of the Data Network

Pilot to overcome the Challenges of „over"-Specification in the Procurement of new Trains

The Swiss Federal Railways is also responsible for procurement, replacement and put in service of new trains through the public tendering process. These procurements are massive investments, often more than $1 billion, which using traditional procurement approach (RfI/RfP) creates very long lead times. In addition, the states have new financial efficiency targets and began to question the overhead costs associated with such multi-year programs. The Swiss Federal Railways, however, had little experience applying Agile in Procurement and struggled to more efficiently replace their rolling stock fleets. Lean Agile Procurement (LAP) offered promising solutions to all these challenges, risks and concerns.

Recognizing the promising benefits of LAP, management decided to pilot LAP for just one system of the trains - the sanitary systems. This provided a narrower focus that ensured, the team wouldn't be overwhelmed by the sheer complexity of the overall train and all its systems. In essence, it offered an opportunity to focus and learn quickly with limited risk. However, to assume that the sanitary systems on Swiss trains are simple would be a wrong assumption. Swiss trains sanitary solutions have been fitted with something known as, „on-wheel wastewater treatment systems" that recycle greywater at a cost of approximately $1 million each. Therefore, they are quite complex.

Goals

The mission of the pilot was to leverage and quickly validate if the team could simplify and improve the efficiency of the specification process for the sanitary system.

- A potentially publishable specification of the sanitary system was available
- Learnings were made available (including impact on lead times through the current state public tender procedure, including overhead costs, and quality of specifications, etc)

Approach & Timing

The pilot was designed to test the differences between a traditional specification approach and an

Agile approach. The leadership asked for a short-term focused and incremental pilot implementation using LAP. At this stage it wasn't clear if and how we would use the results of this pilot and how many patterns of LAP we would apply.

It all started, as usual, with a kick-off workshop meeting where we invited all the key stakeholders as well as the current and potential new members of the pilot team. During the workshop we co-created the goals, set the guardrails and empowered the team. All the information was captured on the canvas.

We also asked all participants about their key concerns, and these were some they reported:

- The current culture vs. a disruptive approach such as LAP
- The process of how and what we would specify
- The alignment of all internal stakeholders
- ..

By the end of the kick-off workshop, the cross-functional team was set up and ready to go. In our first workshop session as a team, we reviewed the basics of the LAP in more detail in order to co-create a joint strategy moving forward. The current sanitation specifications were taken from one of the most recent public tenders. The team tried to take advantage of this approach, with the result that they had to manage several hundred specifications just for the sanitary system. This meant thousands of specifications for the whole train. There was no doubt that the pilot could bring some benefits in terms of simplification and streamlining. Based on the current specifications, the effort to prepare a bid would be enormous. It was recognized, that these standard specifications made sense for large projects with fleets of off-the-shelf trains. However, our task was to question the „over"-specification for the smaller procurement case, with some very specific needs.

While challenging the status quo, we started with the negative impacts of over-specification. The team came up with pre-procurement, procurement and post-procurement impacts.

Some obvious examples were and still are:

- **overhead costs** to create, manage the scope and prepare it for a public tender on the buyer side (pre-procurement)
- **efforts** to understand, estimate, etc. and come up with a proposal on the buyer side (procurement)

- **lack of innovation** from the vendor/partners because it's exactly this and seems like a fixed scope
- **overhead costs** to assess, accept the delivered product before taking into service, both the vendor and the buyer (post-procurement)
- **prolongation** of schedule, as the development of more detailed specifications takes much longer

In a second step we tried to identify common triggers for over-specification.

- **Different interests** of the various stakeholder groups / system managers
- **Excessive safeguarding** of systems / solutions based on past experience (even formulation of not-requirements).
- **Specifying the solution** instead of outcome, multiple naming with partial contradictions, adoption of standard texts, proofs as requirements or non-measurable requirements. (e.g. "The lines ... must be minimized in their number of bends").

- **Tendering of options**, or late making of strategic decisions (e.g. holding tank vs. bioreactor).
- too many requirements with a **low rating**.

In reviewing the specification we realized that it was too detailed or, in simplistic terms, focused on describing the solution (HOW). We introduced the team to the concept of outcome-based specification using an agile practice called *User Stories*.

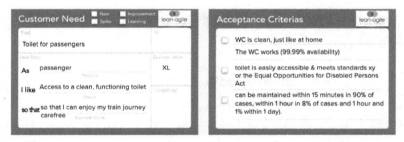

Image source: Swiss Federal Railways

The hypothesis was that a sanitation system could be described with just a few User Stories instead of hundreds of specifications and that they would describe the need from the user's perspective (intended outcome). The team agreed and we started to apply LAP's PREPARATION pattern. We started by identifying the key stakeholder groups / personas for the sanitation system and invited the key representatives to a customer-centered workshop. We wanted the users to directly review and evaluate the current train in order to co-create and develop the needs. The team was responsible for organizing this 4-hour workshop and brought their ideas and questions to the table. The other critical component was that the venue for the workshop was at the actual train, enabling the customers and key stakeholders to „walk through" and experience usability and leverage an actual train to help to clearly communicate their needs.

The results were fantastic. In just 4 hours, we all aligned ourselves with the business objectives, shared our ideas and captured the needs of the user representatives. A task that would have taken the team weeks to complete using a traditional approach. We also tapped into the collective intelligence of all these internal experts to ask the strategic question if the current complex „on-wheel wastewater treatment system" was the best approach moving forward.

The team faced the challenge that required a strategic decision in order to avoid doubling their efforts in the sanitation system specification. The options were:

A) A tank

B) A sewage treatment plant (also called bioreactor)

There was an opportunity to eliminate at least one option of requirement. Within 15 minutes we had a clear recommendation. All the experts agreed that a tank would be much more appropriate and easy to maintain (fresh water refill / gray water discharge). The team also gained additional insight into the plant's current challenges, which were not well known.

One of the key passenger issues that was raised and discussed concerned the quantity and availability of the toilets on the commuter train. There's usually only one toilet on a train, and if it's not working, it's a bad customer experience. We asked the experts what were the main reasons for this and to our surprise, the main reason was a blockage in the pipe. We asked the experts for their recommendation and they came up with a simple solution - increase the diameter of the pipe. Even if the whole workshop had been overhead, these two insights were very important for the sourcing case and any future sourcing case!

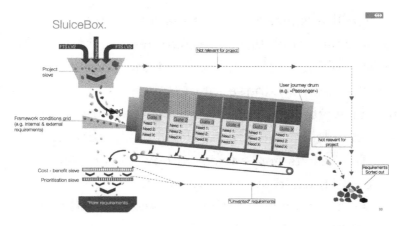

Image source: Swiss Federal Railways

After processing all the input, the team asked themselves what to do with it. The feeling was that we hadn't come up with anything new that wasn't already specified. I didn't question this, but reminded them of the challenges of over-specification. I inspired them by asking what if we just used the few user stories/customer needs instead. To my surprise, one of the team replied that 10-15 years ago, tender documents wouldn't have been more than 10-20 pages long! The team members were divided on how to proceed, until one of them had the idea of mapping the needs gathered in the workshop against the current specifications for validation and optimization. This way they could still use the historical knowledge and minimize the risk of forgetting anything important. The approach was even nicknamed the "sluice box". The team started to collaboratively filter the current requirements based on the needs, objectives, conditions of the sourcing case, etc. It turned out that a lot of standards and requirements were repeated that could have been referenced only once at a higher level of abstraction.

The results and advice on how to proceed were reported back to the management.

As a final activity of the pilot, we invested 4 hours in a "what if ..." workshop. This was designed to explore the possibilities and unspoken ideas of all the team members if there weren't any barriers.

Image source: Swiss Federal Railways

We started by creating a safe space where any idea - even the weirdest - was welcome. The team even set up a prize for the winning idea as an added incentive. So the team members brainstormed all their ideas. After the presentation, we assigned them to the four quadrants with the two scales of impact and feasibility. Finally, the team rated the best ideas in the quadrant high impact / high feasibility and the winner. The best idea was very powerful, but stupidly simple - to contact a small private railway operator in Switzerland to share how they approach such procurement cases on a very limited budget.

Today I start with such an exercise when the culture demands it.

Metrics

In the pilot of the Swiss Federal Railways, the team reported success based on the following key metrics:

- **44% Reduction of specifications** with the „sluice box" approach
- **Higher quality** of specifications with less contradictions
- **Increased attractiveness** of the technical specifications and reducing the accompanying costs, also for follow-up projects.
- **Increased satisfaction** of team and involved stakeholders

The pilot was able to demonstrate how a streamlining of the technical specifications can be achieved with a positive impact for the Swiss Federal Railways and the provider. The pilot recommends that the significant streamlining of the data in the tool for future procurement projects be pushed forward.

Business Outcome

Beside the metrics the Swiss Federal Railways reported the following business outcomes applying Lean-Agile Procurement:

- Increased business value through continuous user involvement, and direct fact to face communication and co-creation e.g. during the customer workshop and weekly public reviews.
- Staffing and empowering the cross-functional team, resulting in a significant reduction in the lead time to complete the work. The team had end-to-end skills for the selected system specification.
- The customer-centric workshop also enabled the team to collaboratively discover and understand, in just 4 hours, the social and technical risks by validating the given

specifications, future needs and leveraging open-ended questions.

- Based on the customer-driven needs, the team jointly designed a new outcome-based specification strategy that significantly reduced the overall risk, while maximizing customer value.

- The „sluice box" not only helped to reduce and improve the requirements for this sourcing case, but for all future cases as the results were fed back into the tool.

Pilot for the Procurement of a customized Software for the Visualization of the Data Network

Swiss Federal Railways isn't just a mobility company, it's also a telecommunications company with its own data and mobile network for train management and beyond. In the past, all network components such as routers, switches, cabling, etc. were documented in individual files. The sheer number of devices, as well as the increased likelihood of outdated designs, increased the risk that the maintenance and support organization would not be able to find the right device in time to resolve operational issues.

APP to View the Network / Components

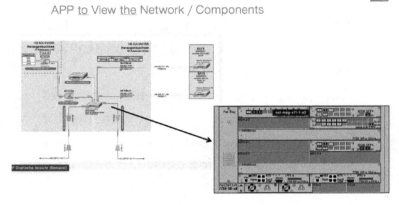

Image Source: Swiss Federal Railways

In the past, a first attempt to introduce software failed. The real-time visualization of thousands of nodes was too much of a challenge. The LAP collaborative approach of bringing together internal and external experts to co-create strategies to overcome this complexity seemed the only way out of the current dilemma.

Goals

The mission of the pilot was to evaluate a new mobile application that visualizes all physical network elements and their connections between sites (over 20,000 elements).

- All elements of the network can be visualized in **real time** using geospatial techniques.
- **Performance is less than 2 seconds** to get a quick overview in just a few clicks
- New App is in service in less than 9 months (including public tender)

Approach & Timing

To gain speed and focus, a cross-functional team was set up applying LAP. During the development of a common sourcing strategy, 2 potential vendor/partners/solutions were shortlisted. One with a preferred vendor/partner and a trusted solution and the other with an internal development team used to 3D programming. The team decided to go with the off-the-shelf solution first and invited the vendor/partner directly to a Big Room Workshop. Together we explored the specific requirements of the solution and the capabilities of the trusted software. After less than an hour, we both concluded that the software was not fit for purpose. So the team turned to plan

B), the internal software team. Again the team invited them to a four hour Big Room workshop and this time we developed a roadmap, negotiated the Agile contract based on an agreed solution. The engineers were very honest about the performance risk with over 20,000 data points. The internal development team acknowledged the risk and proposed 2 solutions. „One of which would certainly work", they said.

Image Source: Swiss Federal Railways

In other words, the roadmap was adjusted based on the biggest known risks, the performance of the solution. And the joint delivery team started with a short proof of concept (PoC) to test the hypotheses.

After these tests, the appropriate software framework was selected and delivery of the entire application began.

Metrics

In the pilot of the Swiss Federal Railways sourcing case, the team reported success based on the following key metrics:

- **400% Improvement in Time-to-Market** compared to a traditional public tendering
- **90% Risk Reduction** through early involvement of technical specialists
- **100% Business Value** through an outcome-based Specification
- **9 out of 10 Recommendation Rate** from team, the involved stakeholders and vendor/partners

Business Outcome

Beside the metrics the Swiss Federal Railways reported the following business outcomes applying Lean-Agile Procurement:

- Increased business value through continuous user involvement, and direct face-to-face communication and co-creation e.g. during the customer workshop and weekly public reviews.
- Staffed and empowered the cross-functional team, significantly reducing the lead time to complete the work. The team had end-to-end decision capability to make any decision within the given constraints
- The Big Room Workshop (s) enabled the team to collaboratively discover the best solution together with the invited vendor/ partners and leveraging open-ended questions.
- The sourcing strategy of looking for pre-defined internal and external preferred solutions/partners massively shortened the lead time as opposed to an open public tender

General Observations, Recommendations & Opportunities for Government Procurement

Public procurement represents roughly 14% of the EU GDP with a value of approximately EUR 1.8 trillion (2015 data). It is not only a crucial pillar of strategic governance and service delivery, but also a key economic activity. If used strategically, public procurement can improve the competitiveness of market economies, as well as help deliver major policy outcomes in response to today's societal and economic challenges, especially when it comes to creating sustainable growth and jobs.[4]

In this chapter, we'll focus on government procurement. Specifically sharing our experience, observations, and recommendations regarding how future strategic procurement should be approached in

---

[4]   OECD Public Procurement - https://www.oecd.org/gov/public-procurement/country-projects/public-procurement-and-cohesion-policy-objectives/

government procurement, or any highly regulated environments.

Who is the Customer in Government?

Everyone agrees that the states involved, and ultimately their citizen is the real customers in government. However, the public sector is more complicated, particularly when it comes to procurement. Key stakeholders such as politicians, lobbyists and lobby groups come into play. In addition, the public sector by its nature and design demands additional accountability and transparency. This has historically been accomplished by very non-agile, rigid, hierarchical bureaucracies, where decision-making and oversight are top down.

The traditional public sector stove-piped organizational design where each group is accountable for their respective part, tends to constrain end-to-end, or systems based accountabilities that are often more difficult to achieve.

Our observation is that procurement is far too limited to the scope, encompassing only the window from post business case creation to contract award.

Post-contract award accountabilities are either passed off to internal "operations", or to a 3rd party for outsourced services. In both cases the assumptions that were documented in the planning phase, are often tested for the first time during implementation. In contractually bound outsourced procurements, wrong or unknown assumptions are managed in the post contract, implementation phase through the "change management" and contract renegotiation process. This tends to balloon project costs and schedules.

The above system, and approach was able to function reasonably well for commodity purchasing, that has few to no assumptions. However, strategic procurements required for public sector procurement need a much different approach. Lastly, as outlined by the opening quote, the majority of strategic procurements within a country are generated by the public sector, therefore even small improvements here, can have significant national economic and social impacts.

Our Recommendations

All of the success stories have shown, that a critical success factor is to involve the key people from the team and stakeholders in setting the context from the start. During the execution of the sourcing case, customer representatives from the public sector jurisdiction are involved in key events such as kickoff/empowerment, sprint reviews, obstacle removal, decision making related to business objectives/guardrails. For example, for the sourcing of new trains this included: conversation about the larger context or the impact on society, current development plans of the region, future commuter movement flows along the train route, what are the environmental objectives, and more. All are important inputs to the sourcing case in government procurement. The Karlstad Hospital case showed the positive impact of having key people, engaged early to establish the outcomes, economics and timing.

Where parliamentarians and/or steering committees have the final say, it's also recommended that the Agile delivery team be empowered to at least make a recommendation. However, in the majority of cases in the Public Sector, the political level should be focused on the intended outcomes and ensure that there is an iterative framework with tight feedback loops to ensure progress is being made toward those outcomes.

Outcome-based Tender, Really?

Public tenders with several thousand specifications are not uncommon. Needless to say, there is significant time and effort for the buyer side to write them, and the supply side to understand and estimate them. In addition, a written document leaves considerable room for interpretation, as often both sides consider the RfX document as an initial draft contract open to interpretation. As shown in the story with the Swiss Federal Railways these specification documents, often constrain the process and provide little additional value. As previously mentioned, the over-specification approach, results in a **lose-lose scenario** for all parties and stakeholders. Another underestimated challenge is when these specifications are over prescriptive. They are more focused on the solution, or the HOW, which severely limits vendor/partners ability to share their innovative solutions, ideas and intellectual property (IP).

Our Recommendations

It's critical to have customer-centric workshops with actual customer representatives on the subject in attendance to understand the key needs that bring value. This pattern was repeated over and over with toilets on the trains, the nurses, and the utility customers with the smart meters. This customer engagement is essential in order to validate the assumptions early in the process.

Documentation in a truly outcome-based approach could become much leaner, more manageable and improve the quality of the communications between buyer and vendor/partner. Our experience with actual LAP implementations has shown that outcome-based tenders of 10-20 pages are quite feasible, even for complex public tenders such as new trains. This new WHY and WHAT focused approach, combined with open and transparent face to face interactions, can improve alignment by orders of magnitude.

Further, this approach enables healthy, open, fair and transparent coopetition (collaboration+competition) between multiple vendors/partners. Lastly, since an outcome-based approach focuses on WHAT and not HOW, it doesn't require vendor/partners to share confidential information, again ensuring a fair, open and transparent procurement.

Of course, this would require an adapted procurement strategy to overcome the risk of a less detailed scope. Please refer to the chapter "How to Source new Trains, a $1BN Investment, applying LAP Full stack?-From Fairytales to Agile".

Do we maximize Value for Tax-paying Citizens?

One of the key themes of the previous chapters poses the question as how to optimize value for taxpaying citizens - let's be very self-critical for a moment.

> „If we asked a Mercedes garage to find us the best car, we'd always get a Mercedes."
> – Mirko Kleiner

However, if we look at the problem from an outcomes-basis versus a solution basis, in a sourcing of new trains, for example, it becomes more about the mobility of citizens over a specific geography. When we start thinking in this way, a variety of solutions come to mind, such as:

- Light-rail trains
- Trams
- Buses
- Self-driving taxis
- etc

Our Recommendations

In the initial stages of future projects and initiatives, it's imperative to start with WHY - specifically, an outcome and an impact-based view of the business objectives. This will lead to a significantly different procurement strategy, and in some cases with a potentially different approach to procurement authority. In addition, this approach would expose other important considerations such as the projected broader impacts on society and the environment for example.

As we discussed with the leadership of the Swiss Federal Railways, a custom train is one of the most expensive solutions. Early in the project, the potential considerations for solutions should not be limited to the current existing or legacy solutions of the firm. In this case of the Swiss Federal Railways, light rail trains or buses and other forms of transportation should be considered, even if they don't currently offer these solutions. From our preliminary discussions we all agreed that there are much cheaper and faster transportation solutions available, that had not been really considered.

Politics, Innovation & Resistance

One insight that was discovered during several projects with various governments was that the detailed specification was driven by accountability for day-2 maintenance and support. The Swiss Federal

Railways, for example, were accountable for day 2 support and operations of trains after delivery. With this in mind, it's understandable that the trains were specified in great detail to mitigate the risk related to poor maintenance and durability.

Also, as mentioned at the beginning of this section, the organizational design divided the work such that plan-build-and deploy and operate were separate divisions with divisional accountabilities, versus organizing in such a way for systemic end-to-end outcome-based accountabilities.

Therefore, what would be the impact of taking a systems-based approach?

What would happen, for example, if we leveraged an outsourced solution for day 2 maintenance and support on the basis of contractual performance-based service levels? Or what if the vendor/ partners have skin in the game like in the Karlstad Hospital case? Would this improve the lead time for procurement, delivery lead time and the service quality levels? Unfortunately , these alternatives were often never considered.

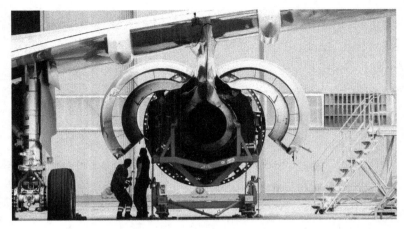

Image source: *thetimes.co.uk*

The full service model where the vendor/partner takes on this greater level of accountability is not new. In the aerospace industry, for example, Rolls-Royce set a new global standard years ago with subscription-based payment for aircraft turbines. In other words, airlines pay per hour in the air, everything else is included in the price. Another more specific example is the Austrian Federal Railways, which has a Service Level Agreement (SLA) for cleaning services. These approaches work, as long as they are outcomes based and iterative in the early stages.

We often observed that government employees immediately stop talking about it because outsourcing was culturally unthinkable. In some cases, from an outcomes-based perspective, the internal procurement team is actually in a conflict of interest situation. To be fair, such situations are not limited to the public sector, as we have found them in the private sector as well. These are some of the examples of the challenges we've experienced with politics and resistance to innovative ideas.

Our Recommendations

Leadership should actively foster an open culture where anything is possible within the given objectives and guard rails, throughout the initiative, but specifically at the initial phase. Often we experience long discussions about the idea of outsourcing maintenance, and the assumed fear of redundancies is often the driving force behind the resistance.

We would also recommend that the leadership take an evidenced-based approach. Often decisions are made with little or no evidence to support them. This is important before and during the case. Often political resistance is based on fear, so evidence and implementation experience, such as small pilots or experiments provide real evidence for better leadership choices and often create consensus regarding the way forward.

In the "what if" workshop, the team came up with a great idea: Taking into account the social responsibility of a Swiss Federal Railway, the winning bidder would have access to the current facilities and staff, but would have to be engaged with the current maintenance staff as well.

Minimizing Risk through Options: Isn't that incremental Supply? - A Supplier's point of view

When the expenditure is high government agencies often attempt to mitigate risk by asking for options. For example, they might order the first 10 trains with options to order 10, 20, etc. more. Initially, this seems to make sense, at least from a buyer's perspective, however, there are several challenges associated with this sourcing strategy. The effort and costs required by the vendor to respond to the tender are the same regardless of the volume of trains ordered. Therefore, if the guaranteed order size is small to begin with, this shifts the risk to the vendors.

Options require additional specifications, which require additional time and effort to create, and publish. From a citizen/passenger point of view, this latency increases the risk of obsolete specifications, that omit key features such as WiFi, and computer power sockets for example. In today's world where technology is changing at unprecedented rates, the time from initial idea to implementation and validation of sourcing cases is critical for the procurement to create actual business value. For example, if the procurement takes 3 years to complete, and another option is taken by the buyer after 10 years, the resulting trains will be 13 years old!

Lastly, it's important to "do the right things, and also to do those things right". In lean it's important to eliminate waste, therefore, rather than having multiple options, perhaps in many cases it's more important to reduce the options down to those things that provide value - just do the right things.

The Chief Procurement Officer (CPO) Stadler Rail, a leading Railways Manufacturer, recently said that this latency problem is a major issue for them. Her concern was that after, 13 years, the whole platform of a train had evolved, not just specific components. As a result, they are forced to bid by reinventing an old product, at much higher costs for both buyer and vendor. They even mentioned that the 3rd party supply chain would have evolved significantly over that time horizon, making it difficult to even find components.

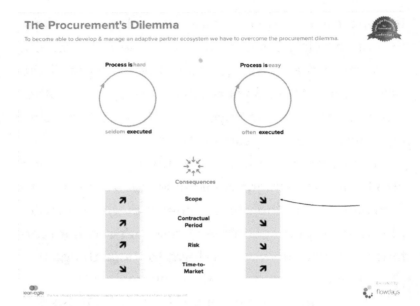

Image source: LAP Alliance, Mirko Kleiner

Our Recommendations

If the train must be a custom solution, then opt for incremental delivery by ordering in small batches where risks will be minimized and assumptions can be validated through iteratively ordering increments. Such an approach may include incremental steps that build on each other such as:

1. Service and maintenance quality & partner(s) capabilities tested on one leased train as an initial validation and evidence collection exercise

240

2. Proven 3D design/prototype to test design capabilities & assumptions of passenger needs
3. Tested wooden prototype of the custom train to test assumptions on passenger needs & look and feel
4. Quality & partner(s) tested on 1st custom train in service
5. 1st batch of trains tested in service & transfer of scale maintenance responsibility
6. etc

In other words, we need to find approaches such as LAP that enable governments to make complex procurement simpler, more frequent and less risky. However, this does require change, and change requires leadership. We have to focus on the most promising hypotheses, that delivers the highest business value while eliminating the biggest risks first.

For more details, see the chapter "How to Source new Trains, a $1BN Investment, applying LAP Full stack?-From Fairytales to Agile".

Culture of fear - What can I do as a Leader?

In every sourcing case with a big investment, but often experienced in highly regulated environments such as government procurement a common observation is a culture of fear. This fear is very real for politicians as there is a significant failure rate on complex procurements and projects in public sector organizations[5]. The resultant bad press, can often result in lost elections or the end of one's political career. This pressure is inevitably transferred to the administration, so that there is much higher scrutiny regarding following given processes. These fears and risks are not restricted to the public sector, corporations also have their share of failure, however, they are often not in the public eye to the same degree.

My personal hypothesis is that because of the huge efforts -roughly estimated several millions of dollars for a case such as the pilot investment per vendor is hard to justify if the project wasn't competed. This might trigger the number of complaints / court cases.

---

[5]   Catalogue of Catastrophe, https://calleam.com/ WTPF/?page_id=3"

Image source: srf.ch

On the other hand the rigid definition of the scope hasn't prevented the Swiss Federal Railways from public criticism, as an organization representing disabled people complaints was recently published in the news. According to the article, disabled people in wheelchairs could not exit the new trains by themselves, because of the entrance ramp was too steeply.

A recent spontaneous survey at a round table of Chief Procurement Officers from different public agencies resulted that in the past 10 years no complaint led to a case. All of them have been sorted out before individually. Btw. The CPO's reported less than 10 complaints in 10 years. So we need to question if this fear is unfounded or self-caused?

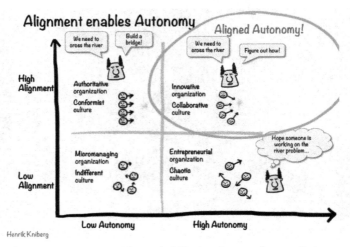

Image source: Henrik Königsberg from Crisp

Our Recommendations

As a leader, it's not easy to influence current culture. Of course, leaders can lead by example, however, it's more powerful to change the organization structure and framework, where you don't have to tell people how to do things as long as these changes serve the organizational and procurement outcomes. Here are three levers for change and some examples:

- Policy
- Structure
- Metrics

Table: Examples how to influence the culture

Tool	Example	Description
Policy	NO Customizing	Organization has to source off-the-shelf solutions / systems / components / services with 1st priority
Policy	Social Outsourcing	Organization is allowed to look for outsourcing partner if social responsibility is ensured
Structure	Max. Overhead costs	Organization is bound to e.g. a max. % of spend budget to overhead costs for government procurement cases
Structure	Max. Lead time	Organization is bound to e.g. a max lead time of 3 months for government procurement case
Metric	Overhead costs	Overhead costs will be tracked transparently per government procurement case
Metric	Lead time	Lead time will be tracked transparently per government procurement case

Metric	Customer Satisfaction	Customer satisfaction will be tracked transparently per government procurement case
Metric	Decision latency	Decision latency will be tracked transparently per strategic decision

The power of a maximum lead time, for example, set by the organization per government procurement case leads to new innovative ways for employees to work within the given rules and regulations.

From Fairytales to Agile: How to Source $1 BN new Trains Investment by Applying LAP Full stack

To illustrate the art of the possible, we've put together an example LAP scenario to overcome the challenges and risks associated with a $1 billion public procurement of new trains.

Disclaimer: LAP is a set of principles, values and patterns for solving complex problems where the context is continually changing. Therefore, the specific context of each sourcing case needs to be considered, at the beginning and throughout the process, in order to understand how to apply the specific LAP tools and process for that instance.

Nevertheless, we hope this will inspire you.

Generally speaking, LAP has its value in all phases of pre-procurement, procurement and post-procurement processes.

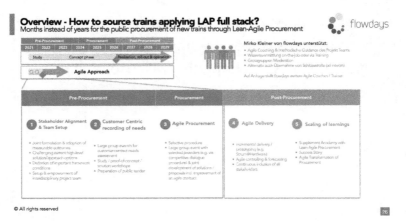

Image source: Mirko Kleiner, flowdays.net

Lead times of up to 5-10 years for replacement of a custom fleet of trains using a traditional procurement approach are quite common. Considering that government procurement in the past has only been 10-20 pages and that it takes only 28 days to produce a single train [6], we need to rebalance things. A common approach in Agile is to fix the time.

---

[6]   Quote by CPO of Stadler Rail

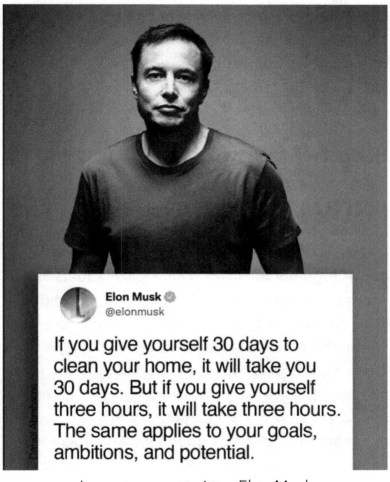

Elon Musk ✅
@elonmusk

If you give yourself 30 days to clean your home, it will take you 30 days. But if you give yourself three hours, it will take three hours. The same applies to your goals, ambitions, and potential.

Image source: twitter, Elon Musk

Under the assumption that time is not variable we start with a recommended maximum pre-procurement and procurement lead times such as, 3 months for example. This establishes entirely new expectations and a completely different mindset for the procurement procedure. It's the team's responsibility to co-create how this will work and they may come up with a similar approach as described in the following.

Step I - Stakeholder Alignment & Team Setup (INITIALIZATION Pattern)

In step (1) Initialization , Lean-Agile Procurement brings together the various core stakeholders. In our Trains case, this would include the key stakeholders from the various States, the Railways and core people on the Agile delivery team for what is typically a 1-day workshop. Bridging the traditional legal terms and compliance with a Lean-Agile Procurement mindset is an important component at this stage. We recommend adding an open-minded procurement expert or lawyer to the team who can optimize the legal components toward the intended outcomes, while ensuring legal compliance.

Phase I - Stakeholder Alignment & Team Setup
In one day the agile delivery team is aligned with the stakeholders and ready to go

flowdays

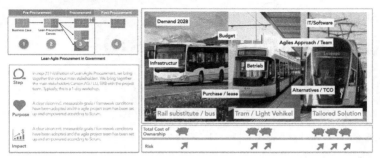

Image source: Mirko Kleiner, flowdays.net

The outcome of this workshop would be for all to align on the context of this case, the vision including measurable business objectives, and the framing conditions. At this point, we want to open the conversation to the broader context including such considerations as the impact on society, current development plans of the region(s), future commuter motion flows along the train route(s), the environmental objectives, etc. All of these kinds of considerations are important inputs to this sourcing case, and it's important to consider them up front. In addition, the Agile delivery team must be empowered at this time so it's cross-function knowledge and expertise can be leveraged for the key recommendations moving forward.

Step II - Customer Centric Needs Analysis (PREPARATION Pattern)

In step (2) Preparation of Lean-Agile Procurement, we prepare the tender and conduct the needs assessment workshops with real passengers, internal experts, etc., among others. Typically this is a 1/2 day workshop per user group. In most cases it's fair to assume that we could gather all needs within less than a week.

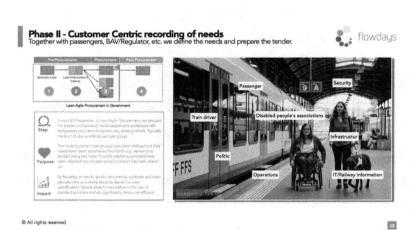

Image source: Mirko Kleiner, flowdays.net

The team would also develop the sourcing strategy. In this sourcing case, a 2-step / selective sourcing process would make the most sense. In the first step, 2-3 vendor/partners are shortlisted, e.g. using profiles. In order to keep the first step as lean as possible for all parties involved, management could define a structure that keeps the tender document outcomes-based and limiting its size to not more than 10 pages.

Such a streamlined, profile-based selection process has been used successfully by the State of Zurich, for example. In their case, all shortlisted providers were awarded and signed a master service agreement similar to a preferred vendor/partner. This ensured global compliance, and allowed them to carry out mini-tenders with a pre-selected set of trusted partners. In addition, the partners could help each other depending on the challenges to be solved, availability, etc.

If there is uncertainty from the vendor/partner community regarding the potential risks of using LAP as a procurement approach, the team could also organize an open industry dialogue, e.g. a 1/2 day workshop, with all interested vendor/partners.

Step III - Agile Procurement (EXECUTION Pattern)

In step (3) the Big Room Workshop of Lean-Agile Procurement, we conduct the procurement in a collaborative way together with all the selected vendor/partners, applying the principles of „fair, open and transparent" to the procurement process. Typically, this is a 2-5 day workshop.

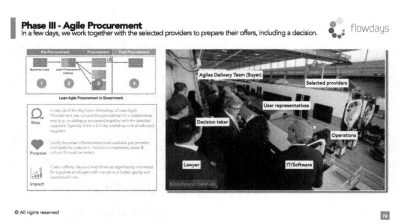

Image source: Mirko Kleiner, flowdays.net

The key outcome of step 3 is to significantly minimize the cost/effort, risks and lead times for vendor/partners and buyers to achieve a contractual agreement, with the same or better quality and better cost/benefit ratio.

To achieve this, we'd suggest inviting the selected suppliers with their most suitable product (in this case a train). The next step would be to walk the train again with internal and external representatives of all key stakeholders. The team would assess the business and cultural fit for each of the respective invited suppliers, addressing outstanding issues, risks and concerns, etc. All these activities are carried out at the same time, as part of the Big Room exercise. Therefore, the Big Room includes vendor partner solution co-creation, as well as evaluation. Government procurement couldn't be more fair, open and transparent! During the train ride, it would also be possible to update the expected lower level outcomes, and simultaneously co-create an Agile contract/proposal with each of the vendor/partners.

In this way, key findings, such as the usability and accessibility of disabled people in wheelchairs, could be addressed before a supplier is awarded a contract.

The legal basis could be the competitive dialogue procedure[7]. In Switzerland, this has so far only been used to improve specifications. However, according to the University of Bern, the law would also allow for the co-creation of a proposal, including the negotiation and joint improvement of a draft Agile contract.

---

[7] Compare with Agreement on Government Procurement (GPA), wto.org

Step IV - Agile Delivery (PEER FEEDBACK pattern)

In step (4) Peer Feedback of Lean-Agile Procurement, we continue to apply the Agile principles, and approaches with collaborative feedback events. Using a collaboration model defined in the Big Room Workshop / empirical controlling & forecasting, we react iteratively to changing requirements (scrum@hardware[8], Lean Startup[9], MvP).

---

[8] Scrum@Hardware by Joe Justice
[9] Lean Startup by Eric Ries

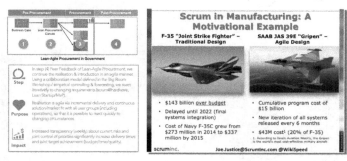

Image source: Mirko Kleiner, flowdays.net

The weekly feedback/review and retrospective events improve the transparency regarding current risks and joint governance of priorities. This significantly improves delivery times and achievement of joint targets (budget/time/quality).

In the case of a newly selected vendor/partner (s), it would be advisable to mitigate risk by first testing the product / train for such attributes as quality and ease of maintenance in service for example. To do this, we'd recommend starting by leasing a train temporarily with integrated maintenance and support in order to collect more evidence, and validate assumptions prior to larger scale investment. This would be the first iteration of delivery, even before we'd start designing the solution for our case. So we'd bring together technical experts, discuss current maintenance challenges from the field, etc.

Image source: RBS.ch / YouTube

Agile development of the design and a wooden prototype, including stakeholder testing, would follow in the next contract before the first batch of mass produced trains was ordered. The risk of misunderstanding the scope would be greatly reduced. Compared with the illustration with the RBS.

The first order to lease a train and design and test a wooden prototype could also be done with multiple vendor/partners.

From our experience, the total lead time could be minimized to 3-6 months if LAP were fully applied, reducing overhead costs, while still delivering higher quality proposals and solution. In addition, it would greatly reduce the risk of complaints. Howev-

258

er, this would require courage, both from those leading and those working together.

Please note: If there was a standard product / train that would suit the purpose, we'd always choose the standard product rather than a custom solution. Another big advantage of outcome-based tendering.

7. Challenges & Solutions Applying Lean-Agile Procurement

Embracing Lean-Agile Procurement introduces a paradigm shift that comes with its share of challenges and innovative solutions. Organizations often face the challenge of aligning traditional procurement mindsets with the dynamic principles of agility. Yet, by fostering a culture of open communication, iterative learning, and cross-functional collaboration, these challenges can transform into stepping stones towards a procurement landscape that thrives on adaptability, customer-centricity, and continuous improvement. These also happen to be the cornerstones of organizational transformation.

Table: Challenges & Solutions applying Lean-Agile Procurement

Challenges	Solutions
Not all core team members are available more than 2 days a week	Don't start with the sourcing case and sort out company priorities at a portfolio level - start with the priorities
A team member likes to be involved just during sourcing but not while delivery	Check first to understand if this person is needed in delivery. If yes, make sure that the person understands the pitfall of unnecessary hand-overs. Worst case look for a replacement. It's volunteers / self-selection versus assignment.
It's not possible to facilitate the Big room workshop as an in person meeting - too expensive to fly everyone	Organize a virtual big room workshop with the same principles of having all parties simultaneously in the same session. Leverage experience Agile coaches / facilitators as this is the next level of maturity

Key stakeholders or leadership aren't really supporting a new LAP sourcing approach	Don't apply LAP until they have understood and committed to support it. PULL is a key principle of Agile, in other words do inspire them to buy-in to LAP. However, don't try to force it.
Leadership is committed to LAP but has concerns that LAP creates a lot of unnecessary overhead	Create a business case / ToC that includes everything and calculate the maximum amount of time & resources (overhead costs) that could be invested. This becomes another framing condition for the team beside timing, budget, etc.
Representatives of key Stakeholder groups are unwilling to participate in e.g. a design thinking workshop	Reflect on the time planned for the workshop and always try to invite everybody simultaneously. As defined in the Kickoff those experts shall be available. Create an impediment, remind the leadership and make it transparent e.g. in the next sprint review. Reinforce the agreed upon outcomes.

For example the first challenge „Not all core team members are available >2 days a week" is something that applies in every LAP Case. The good people are often overbooked and availability is a challenge. However, it is an absolute essential requirement, in order to maximize the speed and efficiency of the core-team members.

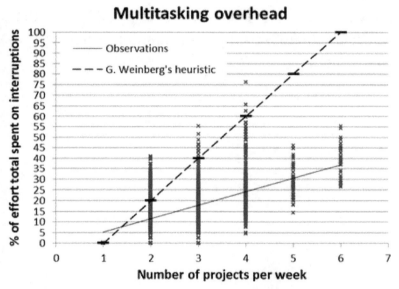

Image source: Book Evaluation of Cross-Project Multitasking in Software Projects by A. Tregubov, Jo Ann Lane & B. Boehm

If these team members are currently working on other higher priority initiatives, we do need to respect that. However, it's better to wait for their full engagement before starting the whole strategic sourcing case than it is to force them to multitask or overbook them.

As the G. Weinberg Heuristics show that there is an inverse proportional relationship between the number of tasks a person does and their personal productivity. For example, a person assigned to 5 projects has a total effectiveness of just 25%. In other words 75% are wasted with content switching between tasks.

8. Implement LAP yourself

Become a Certified LAP Practitioner

Since LAP is a significantly different way of thinking about procurement and strategic sourcing it is highly recommended that team participants get started with our Introductory course in LAP from the LAP Alliance (Certified LAP Practitioner - Credential 1).

The LAP Alliance

Established 2018 the Lean Agile Procurement (LAP) Alliance is a not-for-profit organization of global agile experts that currently disrupt procurement and supply. The LAP Alliance is also a Certification Body and offers in-person and online awareness and advanced certification courses as well as guidance via coaching.

The LAP Alliance offers a comprehensive certification training program to fully develop the capabilities of your people with respect to LAP. These courses will provide you with a solid foundation in LAP principles, enabling you to confidently navigate the complexities of modern procurement.

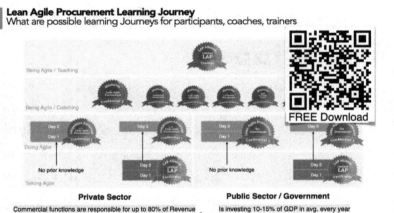

Image Source: LAP Alliance - Learning Journey

The LAP Alliance offers specific Certified LAP Practitioner (Credential 1) workshops designed for the private and public sectors. It includes applicable practices beyond those mentioned in this book and a self-assessment of your procurement organization.

Check out our current workshops or contact one of the Certified LAP Trainers to find out more.

For CPO's, leaders, HR and Procurement Excellence readers, we also offer our training program B2B and include it in your academy.

Agile Coaching and/or a Pilot Project

In addition, seeking coaching and guidance from our experienced practitioners can provide invaluable insights tailored to your unique context. Our Certified LAP Trainers provide Agile coaching to executives, and service line teams, etc.

However, we've found that the greatest learning combined with positive business impact is through the shared experience of implementation. In order to mitigate risk while optimizing learning transfer we recommend organizations start with a pilot implementation of LAP. We offer consultancy, interim leadership, and learning on the job. It's recommended that potential pilot cases are first jointly assessed to ensure optimal achievement of intended outcomes.

Starting small - Apply a pattern

Starting small is often the key to driving meaningful change. You can kick off your LAP implementation by focusing on your existing challenges. For instance, consider applying the Lean Procurement Canvas or utilizing our Heat Map tool to identify areas for improvement.

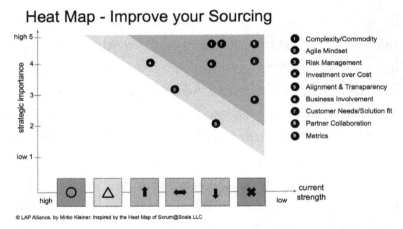

Image source: LAP Alliance - Heat map to assess the agility of a procurement organization

This pragmatic approach allows you to experience the tangible benefits of LAP while progressively extending its principles throughout your procurement processes. By taking these deliberate steps, you can cultivate a culture of agility, collaboration and efficiency within your organization.

Whatever you do, spread the word! The LAP Alliance will co-publish your story on https://www.lean-agile-procurement.com in your name.

9. Current & Future Trends

The current landscape of Lean-Agile Procurement is witnessing a surge in adoption as organizations increasingly recognize its potential to reshape traditional procurement practices. As businesses seek to enhance responsiveness, innovation, and value delivery, Lean-Agile Procurement stands as a guiding light, enabling them to navigate an evolving marketplace with agility and insight.

Looking ahead, the future of Lean-Agile Procurement promises further advances, with a trajectory towards contracts that truly support Agile collaboration, extending current approaches to the entire partner lifecycle toward Agile Partner Management. Various companies from different industries have not only adopted Agile values and principles for their procurement, but are in the process of transforming their entire organization, including governance, processes, policies, etc. Current real case examples are showing that many companies need to collaborate across their network of ecosystem partner companies in order to solve complex problems driven by today's unprecedented rates or change. The combination of these factors is highlighting the critical role for procurement as we move beyond today's static supply chains toward Adaptive Partner Ecosystems. The journey is just starting and as such it is important to start to build the capabilities to manage procurement in this fast-paced environment.

Scaling LAP for small & huge Business Cases

It is important to understand that the cost to scale LAP is proportional to the size of the business case/ Project or project budget. Recently a customer said to me that it seems that there is a significant overhead for a LAP sourcing case with a business case of $ 100,0000. I responded; *„What is the maximum acceptable overhead costs?* And the customer responded that it should not be more than 10% . So the cross-functional team was tasked to find a sourcing strategy within a budget of $ 10,000. Which is equal to 2-3 days internal costs!

The reverse is also true. Large investments, such as a whole new factory or supply chain, can be sliced into different 'product' teams. We've done this successfully with Lightyear[1], a Dutch scale-up bringing the first solar-powered electric car to market. The body-in-white system team, the skeleton of the car, took end-to-end responsibility for the system, including the required partner ecosystem for design, manufacturing, etc.

Agile Partner Management

Agile Partner Management represents a paradigm shift in how organizations engage and collaborate with their vendors and suppliers. Departing from traditional transactional relationships, Agile Partner Management embraces Agile principles to foster a dynamic and iterative approach to collaboration.

---

[1]   https://lightyear.one

Table: Source Mirko Kleiner 2015 - Comparison of traditional and Agile Partner Managment

Agile Partner Management	Traditional Supplier Management
An agile cooperation pursues a partnership at eye level including an adequate learning culture analogous to internal employees	A traditional cooperation seeks a clear demarcation between customer and supplier in order to defuse possible questions of liability and warranty claims.
An agile collaboration is continuously evaluated for validity and follows the agile business goals of the organization	A traditional collaboration is initially created and from then on progress against the initial plan is monitored, without consideration of changing objectives
An agile collaboration can be changed (expanded, reduced) or even stopped by both parties at any time and does not require a notice period	Traditional customer/supplier relationships are rather rigid with notice periods ranging from several months to one year and are automatically extended

Agile collaboration is based on the business benefit/outcome that is generated jointly and shows this measurably	A traditional cooperation is based only on the ability to deliver/output of a supplier
in an agile cooperation both parties want to improve together and therefore accept changing conditions	In a traditional cooperation the supplier should develop further and the customer should benefit from this. Changing framework conditions are perceived as an obstacle

By nurturing closer partnerships, encouraging frequent feedback, and aligning goals, organizations can leverage Agile Partner Management to drive innovation, streamline processes, and create a mutually beneficial ecosystem that thrives on adaptability and shared success.

Image mindmap labels:
- Intake Requests
  - Lean backlog
  - Agile backlog
  - First In First Out (FIFO) queue
- Select Procurement Strategy
  - Lean Agile Procurement (LAP)
  - Traditional procurement (bespoke)
  - Traditional procurement (commodity)
  - Straightforward purchase
  - Automated purchase
- Identify Potential Partners
  - Issue request for proposal (RFP)
  - Issue request for participation (RFP 3.0)
  - Issue request for information (RFI)
  - LAP lean procurement canvas
  - Preferred vendor list
  - Research market
- Identify Partner Strategy
  - Vendor coalition
  - Best-of-breed vendor
- Select Potential Partners
- Choose Collaboration Model
- Develop Working Agreement
- Vendor Management
- Capture Working Agreement
- Choose Contract Model
  - Target price
  - Time and materials (T&M)
- Grow Partner Relationship
  - Co-develop opportunities
  - Co-improve
  - Co-innovate
  - Co-learn
  - Support teams
- End Partner Relationship
  - Cancel contract(s)
  - Complete contract(s)
  - Litigate
- Govern Partnerships
  - Address partnership risks
  - Monitor partner performance (endeavour)
  - Monitor partner performance (overall)
  - Review contract performance
  - Review partner performance
  - Validate purchases

FREE Download

Image source: PMI Disciplined Agile - Agile Vendor Management

To get a first impression of Agile Partner Management, visit the PMI - Disciplined Agile website. Mirko Kleiner co-created Agile Vendor Management with Scott Ambler, co-creator of Disciplined Agile, which was acquired by PMI recently.

In the process goal diagram you'll see that LAP is an important subset of Agile Partner Management. However, it's not the only good practice and the choice of tool depends on the context of the sourcing case at hand.

Agile Contracts / Agreements

Agile Agreements or Contracts mark a departure from conventional rigid contracts, reflecting a dynamic and adaptive approach in procurement. These agreements are crafted to embrace the iterative nature of Agile methodologies, enabling organizations and vendor/partners to collaboratively respond to evolving requirements and market changes. By emphasizing flexibility, continuous communication, and shared accountability, Agile Agreements empower both parties to navigate uncertainties while optimizing value delivery and fostering a stronger foundation for successful project outcomes.

The problem today is that many Agile cross-enterprise delivery teams lack a legal foundation, based on Agile values and principles, to support this kind of Agile collaboration. In addition, there hasn't been a "standard" for what an Agile contract really is and what it isn't. This made it difficult to get the legal community on board, and worse, created even more confusion in the Agile community.

Continuum of traditional & agile Contract types
There's not THE Agile Contract, it needs to be customized based on the current context

Image source: LAP Alliance - Spectrum of Contract types

The simplest solution to defining a standard would be to create a template, or rather THE template, for an Agile contract. This has served us very well in the past where things were predictable. As Agile collaboration tries to embrace uncertainty, each contract has become very contextual. To take it to one extreme, sometimes all we have is a vision of how Artificial Intelligence (AI) could support our business... so time-n-material is the only way to go... a resound-

277

ing NO! But there is a whole spectrum of potential Agile contract types, e.g. driven by the level of risk sharing.

Agile Contract Manifesto

Agile approaches evolved to manage the risks of solving complex problems with high levels of uncertainty. This requires acceptance that contracts are incomplete and evolve over time.

We are uncovering better ways of aligning contracts with agile collaboration by doing it and helping others to do it. Through our work we have come to value:

01   Tangible outcomes more than specified deliverables

02   Clarity and simplicity more than complexity and completeness

03   Adaptive partnerships more than static relationships

04   Joint ownership more than risk-driven accountability

That is, while each element is important, we have found that emphasizing the elements on the left generally leads to better results.

Image source: AgileContactManifesto.org - Values

The only solution for a remaining standard is to take it to the next level of abstraction: Values & Principles. Please welcome the Agile Contract Manifesto (ACM), created by a global group of experts from the agile, business and legal communities. I'm honored to be one of the co-creators.

Principles behind the Agile Contract Manifesto

We observe that these principles are often associated with successful collaboration:

01   Our highest priority is to create a positive outcome for the ultimate customers and for all contracting parties.

02   Collaboration is about more than delivery. The contract is part of the process. Agile collaboration is inclusive, starts before the contract is signed, and extends beyond just the delivery of value.

03   Contract, relationship and governance need to move together. The contract defines the rules of the game. Ensure consistent rules to encourage transparency, integrity, empowerment, autonomy, clarity of purpose, and collaboration.

04   A successful partnership learns and adapts throughout the life of the engagement. The challenge of developing governance is creating enough control while enabling effective, results-oriented work.

05   Minimize the effort spent on non-value producing work. Ensure effort and time focused on indirect activities are optimized and in proportion to the productive activity.

06   Impediments can arise anywhere in a collaboration. A successful result depends on a smooth communication and information flow across boundaries to rapidly identify and respond to issues.

07   Embed mechanisms to manage risk rather than merely allocate risk. Manage risk through transparency, frequent delivery and fast feedback.

08   Ensure clarity on needs and available capabilities. Contract for what is really needed and understand what is really being sold.

09   Continuity and sustainability are essential for long-lived solutions. The team which creates a new solution develops unique knowledge about the product, the technology, risk management, the market, and each other.

10   A good contract is one that anybody can understand.

Image source: AgileContactManifesto.org - Principles

Like an Agile contract, values & principles are contextual. So as a first step, it's a good idea to create a common understanding. The easiest way to do this is by sharing examples. Then you could take an existing Agile contract and evaluate and improve it based on the Agile Contract Manifesto (ACM). It's recommended to involve all parties in this exercise, e.g. Product Owner, Delivery Team Members, Agile Coach or Scrum Master, Lawyer, etc. as the development of this legal foundation will also become a team effort to create maximum ownership and minimize risks at the same time.

Tip: Have a look at the Lean Procurement Canvas, which provides a lot of guidance on how to ask the right questions.

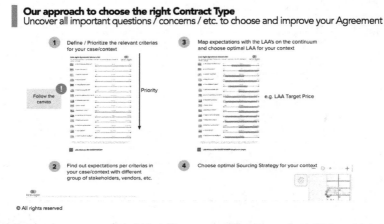

Image source: LAP Alliance - Approach / Criterias to select the optimal contract strategy

In addition to the canvas, we've also developed a set of criteria to help select the optimal contracting strategy or contract type. It's recommended that we extend the current step in the traditional sourcing approach of 'defining the sourcing strategy' to 'defining the contract strategy'.

It's also very important to understand that an Agile contract is not just the Statement of Work (SoW). It includes all parts of a contractual framework such as

280

the Non-Disclosure Agreement (NDA), General Terms & Conditions (GTC), Master Service Agreement (MSA), etc. If you think about your current NDA, for example, you'll agree that there's a lot of room for improvement when it comes to assigning Agile values.

The future of Procurement: From Function to Capability

The future of procurement, and any other function, is undergoing a transformative shift from mere functional roles to that of strategic capabilities. This is a significant shift that influences the entire organizational governance. Pioneering companies like Haier and Buurtzorg have championed this approach by applying ecosystem principles to their internal operations. Haier, for instance, has harnessed platform-based ecosystems to seamlessly connect suppliers, partners, and customers, enabling agile response to market demands. Haier with more than 80,000 employees organized in an Ecosystem of over 4,000 micro-businesses achieved a $2b market value while revenues & profits have grown annually by 20% over the last 10 years.

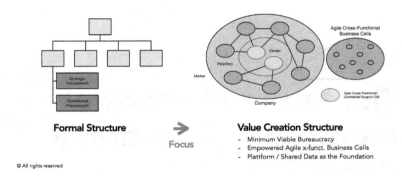

Image source: LAP Alliance - From Function to Capability

Similarly, Buurtzorg, a healthcare provider, has leveraged self-managing teams to empower frontline staff, fostering a decentralized and responsive ecosystem that adapts swiftly to patient needs. Buurtzorg with more than 15,000 employees has one of the highest customer & employee satisfaction without a HR or procurement department. These examples showcase how embracing ecosystem thinking propels procurement beyond traditional boundaries, enhancing agility, innovation, and value across the entire organizational landscape.

Beyond Supply Chain - Adaptive Partner Ecosystem

The concept of "Beyond Supply Chain - Adaptive Partner Ecosystem" heralds a paradigm shift in how organizations approach their supplier relationships. Moving beyond the linear confines of traditional supply chains, this approach envisions a dynamic and interconnected ecosystem of partners and collaborators. By fostering a network that thrives on real-time information sharing, innovation, and co-creation, organizations can adapt swiftly to disruptions, drive continuous improvement, and unlock unparalleled value throughout their entire partner ecosystem.

For years, health authorities had warned of a pandemic. Yet when COVID-19 hit us, the world was largely unprepared. In these challenging conditions, 'agility' took many forms, but perhaps the most interesting was the critical search for a vaccine that would allow a return to 'normal' economic and social activity.

„When the need is urgent, there's no time for contracts. The alliance between BioNtech, Pfizer and Fosun Pharma to develop the COVID19 Vaccine was founded on trust-based collaboration."
— **Ugur Sahin**, *CEO Biotech*

The story behind the Pfizer vaccine, and in particular the co-creation between BioNTech, Pfizer and Fosun, is a lesson in trust, but more importantly, trust embedded in a formal structure. Ugur Sahin, CEO of BioNTech, was one of the CEOs who "co-created the commercial framework for truly agile development involving supply networks or ecosystems"[2].

„The border of the company is not important if you can help create Value for user."
— **Tan Lixia**, *CFO Haier*

With LAP, we have developed the ingredients to find, select and build Adaptive Partner Ecosystems much faster than is possible today. Inspired by progressive

---

2   Source: World Commerce & Contracting - Tim Cummins

examples like Haier and Buurtzorg, we're developing LAP beyond sourcing - stay tuned!